With my greetings and
Compliments.

L. J. Coffman

To

Reverend Julius W. Hann

THE STATE UNIVERSITY
ITS WORK AND PROBLEMS

THE STATE UNIVERSITY
ITS WORK AND PROBLEMS

A SELECTION FROM ADDRESSES
DELIVERED BETWEEN 1921 AND 1933

═══════════════[BY]═══════════════

LOTUS D. COFFMAN

PRESIDENT OF THE
UNIVERSITY OF MINNESOTA

LONDON · HUMPHREY MILFORD · OXFORD UNIVERSITY PRESS
THE UNIVERSITY OF MINNESOTA PRESS
MINNEAPOLIS

Let those who wish to be political and industrial leaders receive the support they deserve. As for me, I should prefer to be known in the years to come as one who stood in these days for strengthening rather than weakening education; as one who helped to modify and adjust it to meet the demands of new problems and to prepare for a new day; as one who has not discarded the great tradition of America that universal education is essential to public welfare and that a highly educated leadership is basic to human progress.

President's Report, *1932*

ACKNOWLEDGMENTS

The Committee on the Press of the University of Minnesota, under whose direction this volume was prepared, make grateful acknowledgment to the publishers of their permission to reprint those addresses which have already appeared in periodicals and books: the Inaugural Address in *School and Society* and in *The University and the Commonwealth* (University of Minnesota, 1921); Freedom of Teaching and Conflicting Governmental Philosophies in *School and Society;* The Obligation of the State University to the Social Order in *School and Society* and in *The Obligation of Universities to the Social Order* (New York University Press, 1933); The State University: Its Relation to Public Education in the *Journal of the National Education Association;* Flexner and the State University in the *Journal of Higher Education;* Two Ways of Improving the State Universities in the *Educational Record;* The Relation of the University to the State in *Minnesota Chats;* Thinking in Terms of Tomorrow in the *Minnesota Alumni Weekly;* Educational Trends in the University of Minnesota in *The Changing Educational World* (University of Minnesota Press, 1931); An Address on the Fiftieth Anniversary of the Founding of the University of North Dakota in the *Quarterly Journal of the University*

ACKNOWLEDGMENTS

of North Dakota; and The Efficacy of the Depression in Promoting Self-Examination as Chapter II in *Needed Readjustments in Higher Education* (Proceedings of the Institute for Administrative Officers of Higher Institutions, Volume V, University of Chicago Press, 1933).

The papers included in this volume were selected as being among the most representative of President Coffman's public addresses, and as embodying his democratic philosophy of American higher education.

CONTENTS

I. INAUGURAL ADDRESS 1

II. FREEDOM OF TEACHING................. 26

III. THE STATE UNIVERSITY: ITS RELATION TO
PUBLIC EDUCATION 38

IV. THE RESPONSIBILITY OF HIGHER INSTITU-
TIONS OF LEARNING FOR THE DEVELOPMENT
OF EDUCATION 60

V. THE RELATION OF THE UNIVERSITY TO THE
STATE 80

VI. THE UNIVERSITY AND THE MODERN WORLD   94

VII. TWO WAYS OF IMPROVING THE STATE UNI-
VERSITIES 115

VIII. EDUCATIONAL TRENDS IN THE UNIVERSITY OF
MINNESOTA 132

IX. ADULT EDUCATION 148

X. FLEXNER AND THE STATE UNIVERSITY...... 155

XI. EDUCATION AND THE DEPRESSION.......... 164

XII. THINKING IN TERMS OF TOMORROW....... 183

ix

CONTENTS

XIII. The Obligation of the State University to the Social Order................... 201

XIV. An Address on the Fiftieth Anniversary of the Founding of the University of North Dakota........................ 217

XV. Conflicting Governmental Philosophies 235

XVI. The Efficacy of the Depression in Promoting Self-Examination.............. 254

ADDRESSES

ADDRESS ON THE OCCASION OF HIS
INAUGURATION AS PRESIDENT OF
THE UNIVERSITY OF MINNESOTA

Minneapolis, May 13, 1921

T HE history of public education in America is a story of achievement. To the student of education it reads like romance. No adequate account of it has ever been written. Some day someone who knows how to wield a master's pen will attempt it, and the greatest epic of civilization will be produced. To recount the struggles of a free people to establish a system of popular education, which in its infancy bore the stigma of poverty and charity but in latter days is the expression of the hopes and ambitions, the faiths and aspirations, of the proud descendants of that people, is a task worthy of the noblest and most gifted mind. To recount the struggles of a people to preserve and perpetuate the principles of freedom of worship, the right of assembly, trial by one's peers, and the opportunity for fair discussion is to retell the story of American education, for through it, and only through it, can we insure an intelligent and wise application of these inalienable principles. Both the sanctity and the meaning of our political institutions rest in the final analysis upon the kinds of schools we maintain.

This school system of ours did not spring into existence full grown. It is the product of evolution. Its roots lie far back in the past. From the beginning it has been regarded as society's most sensitive agent for saving time and labor and also as a highly specialized instrument consciously organized to provide training in citizenship. Thomas Jefferson clearly recognized the importance of this latter consideration. When he declared that a free government cannot endure without public education, he gave a mighty impetus to its cause. Successful public schools everywhere became radiant points of imitation. The right of sovereignty changed from groups that voluntarily taxed themselves to groups that compulsorily taxed themselves.

From then until now, decade after decade, the common schools have advanced with uncertain and halting steps. Could we have looked into the future then as we can examine history now, we should have known that the future of the schools was secure, for their foundations were rooted in the idealism of a people who cherished not merely the right to worship God according to the dictates of their own conscience, but also the privilege of educating their children in accordance with the principles of freedom and equality of opportunity. These are not principles to be exercised without discretion. They are something to be achieved. The right of free worship and equality of political opportunity have almost, if not quite, been realized in this country. But there are other types of liberty for which many are struggling that have not yet been commonly accepted. They are still in the process of formulation. Even intellectual liberty, that is, the right to discover truth and to tell the whole truth in order that the truth may make us free, is not universally received and is not always treated with the cordiality that it deserves, yet it is the only stimulus to science and the only true basis of progress.

The fundamental tenets of popular education in America have never contemplated aristocratic forms of education, the cultivation of class interests, nor the protection of special privileges. On the contrary, since the middle of the nineteenth century the common schools — the product of that proud, new tradition that all property shall be taxed for the education of all children — have been universally regarded as the servant of everyone, not the servant of a few.

Almost contemporaneously with the establishment of a system of common schools our forefathers began to enact compulsory education laws, fixing the upper age limit in some instances as high as fourteen. Apparently these pioneers held that the level of trained intelligence needed by all the people for the solution of the problems of that day and generation should be graduation from the common schools. Life was comparatively simple, and its problems easy of solution. On the other hand, there rested deep in the hearts of the common people the firm conviction that a certain amount of general training was necessary to insure mutual understanding and social intercourse. These pioneers understood that a common education is one of the first requirements of neighborliness, that it tends to loosen the bonds of selfishness and makes it easier for men to live together, to work and to play together.

That enormous progress has been made in general education in America is shown by the fact that in 1840 the total amount of education received by the average citizen during his entire lifetime was 208 days. According to present standards, this nation, educationally speaking, was in 1840 a low second grade nation. By 1870 the total amount of schooling received by the average citizen had been increased to 582 days. We had reached a new level – the level of a high third grade. Today the average citizen receives a little over 1,200 days of schooling. We are now a high sixth, or a low seventh grade nation.

Why this change? Because the problems of each succeeding generation have been more difficult than

4

those of the preceding generation. Furthermore, the problems have grown more political, social, and spiritual in character. Our forefathers two generations ago understood that social and political problems are not altogether economic but also intellectual and spiritual. To them a carpenter was not a carpenter merely but a citizen as well. The working man has long suspected that the man who knows possesses some secret influence or power that is being denied the worker. Some have thought that power was money and consequently have sought higher wages. Others have thought it was political prestige and consequently have sought political preferment. But most of them have learned that the secret lies in education. As a result the doors of the schools have been opened to the children of men on every economic level. Every time any class has secured greater political rights it has demanded more education, and it has always obtained it. The constant extension of education to lower economic levels epitomizes the struggle of the race for human freedom. It is this struggle of the masses to secure an education, combined with their ability to profit by it and to use it intelligently, that gives us confidence in the ultimate outcome and integrity of democracy. Everyone recognizes that such education is expensive, but the expense is insignificant in comparison with the enormous gain society receives from it.

The period during which the common school system was developed throughout the nation was that between 1840 and 1855. From 1840 to 1870 much of the secondary education was provided in private schools, generally known as seminaries or academies. Gradually since then these private schools have been superseded by the public high school. This change came partly because the whole social organism was increasing in complexity and its problems in intricacy and variety. The population was growing rapidly. Thousands upon thousands of foreigners were passing through the immigration gates. Lines of communication were multiplying. Newspapers and books were more easily available. Acute political, social, and industrial issues arising out of the Civil War and our industrial expansion remained unsolved. The dark days of reconstruction dragged on. Although there seemed to be good ground for discouragement, the men of that day did not regard the situation as hopeless. Their idealism did not become distorted, nor did they lose faith in their institutions. They did what every generation of patriots has done — they made way for liberty by providing more education. High school education, available to the children of all men, became their goal. They sacrificed that the next generation might have a better intellectual equipment than they had had. Right in the midst of this period of great economic and spiritual depression the University of Minnesota was founded.

Such is the history of all human progress. Each succeeding generation profits by the sacrifices of the preceding generations. These sacrifices always point in the direction of greater service to mankind. All too frequently do we forget that there is human ethics in human progress, that the comforts we enjoy, the satisfactions we have, the privileges we possess, all came because men who received but a few days of schooling during their lifetime were willing to pay a heavy price for us. There is a moral in this for the present generation which I shall not press.

Long before the high school became an integral part of the established school system, many of the states created universities, which in the course of time articulated with the public schools and became a part of them. There are still a few skeptics who maintain that a state university should be separate and independent of the public schools. They would locate it on some Mount Olympus or sequester it in some secret place far from the sordid marts of trade and the buzzing confusion of the social and political worlds. Scholarship, in their opinion, should not be contaminated by contact with the activities of everyday life. A wall with a wide and deep moat should separate the university from the high school, and only the very elect, the superlatively gifted, should be permitted to cross the bridge and enter the gate. This is the philosophy of other days. The philosophy of today points to a system of state-supported public education, beginning with the lowest primary grade and extending to the senior year of the university, open equally to all who are competent to profit by it. This philosophy is the foundation rock upon which the entire superstructure of our democratic society is built. Destroy it, and democracy will fall. Cling to it, and democracy will survive.

The early state universities were modest in their claims. They were what Dr. Folwell would call "good schools." A varied curriculum was not required. Many of the instructors were great teachers. They enjoyed intimate personal relations with their students. The students were accepted as a part of the community. Student life was conducive to good scholarship. Those were the days when great personalities cast their shadows far into the future. A few distinguished leaders like Dr. Folwell and Dr. Northrop caught a vision of what universities were to become. These empire builders saw the institution over which they presided growing in size and in influence. New courses were introduced, the curricula were revised and expanded; more instructors were secured; the contact between students and staff became less intimate. From an institutional point of view these changes brought both gains and losses. With the influx of students, dormitories began to be substituted for homes, convocations for chapel, a more varied and flexible curriculum for the simpler and inelastic ones, student service buildings for boarding clubs; and a more highly specialized staff has taken the place of the one of varied attainments.

To some extent personality has given way to institutionality. By this I do not mean that personality no longer plays a prominent part in the education of university students. On the contrary, it is just as important as it ever was. There is no substitute for it. But it is obvious that the head of a university like Minnesota can no longer know personally all or nearly all of his students. Something has been lost because these warm, intimate, and almost confidential relations which he once enjoyed with his students are no longer possible. But as I have already indicated, every loss has its compensating gain. The president, with his small faculty, has been supplemented by a large faculty; the influence of a few by the influence of many; a few points of contact by many points of contact.

The most important task of the university is that of securing a high-minded, right-minded faculty. What members of the faculty think and believe, what they feel and express, to a greater or less extent transfers itself to and finds expression in the life and thought of the student body. Both individually and collectively the faculty should be imbued with an impelling desire to search for and discover truth. It should be dominated by a reverence for the truth and a high respect for facts, and saturated with human purposes and common human feelings.

A university is a community of scholars; it breathes the spirit of the social order; it is constantly engaged in an attempt to understand the meaning of the age; it inculcates the craft spirit of the profession; it molds character. Every member of a university is a locus of influence. The individual professor still has limitless opportunities to make an impression upon his students. He must play his part; he must accept and express in his daily life the sacred obligation of his profession if the university would serve its true purpose in every respect. He must assist by every act in building that subtle, pervasive, and irresistible force which can best be described by the term "the institutionality of the university." Its constituent elements are the attitudes, the standards, the ideals, and the traditions of the institution.

A university is not an aggregation of individuals merely; it has its social mind, to which every individual contributes. The social mind of a university is not lifeless and inert; it is a powerful dynamic touching the life of faculty and students at every turn. Every stimulus that beats in upon the consciousness of an individual influences him for good or ill. Consequently none but the best influences should prevail in a university. The development of a genuinely wholesome institutionality through the personnel of a high-minded faculty and the associated life of students and faculty in classrooms, libraries, laboratories, commons, union buildings, auditoriums, and stadiums, is the supremely important problem of a modern university. The primary factor of institutionality in a university is studentship, but a university is no longer a school merely. It is a republic of minds, dedicated to the dispassionate consideration of the problems of life and dominated by a wholesome philosophy of helpfulness and mutual good faith. Just as the largest achievement of an individual is himself, so the largest achievement of a university is itself. It makes its own soul – a soul that resides in the best thoughts, the best feelings, and the best conduct of everyone connected with it, and in the attitude toward it of the community in which it is located.

It is a platitude to declare that the primary purpose of a university is to educate, and yet even this platitude needs to be reiterated now and then. Students come to it to master the arts and sciences, to prepare for the professions, or to advance knowledge. The college of liberal arts is presumed to provide that type of liberal training which is necessary for the exercise of intelligent citizenship and a noble use of one's leisure. If one graduates from a university with a love of literature, with the proper standards for evaluating social and political life, if he masters more than one language, if he is equipped to explore new territory in the field of mathematics or the sciences, it is because of the instruction he has received in the college of liberal arts. The college of arts needs no justification; it is the basic college of the university. But it does not exist independent of the other units of the university. Indeed, one of the largest services it renders is the work it does for the other units of the university. Even doctors, dentists, and engineers must be taught English and sometimes physics and chemistry or a foreign language. The college provides this training and in doing so helps to integrate the institution.

Contact with the professional schools has modified the curriculum of the arts college so that much of its work is of vocational nature. It is true that other forces have tended to produce the same result. The bachelor of arts degree, first given as evidence that one was qualified to teach, later in some American institutions assumed to be the insignia of a liberally educated person, is now granted for all sorts of cultural and special lines of work. Special significance is now seldom attached to the degree, but special significance does lie in the fact that the variety of things for which it is given is an indication of the efforts of colleges to liberalize themselves. They have acquired a new meaning and have been touched by a new spirit.

The professional schools have added another element to university life. One studies law to become a lawyer, medicine to become a doctor, engineering to become an engineer. In every case the student has definitely chosen his career. The mere presence of these students in the university means that old apprenticeship forms of training are no longer adequate. The science of the various professions has so far developed and the knowledge has grown so vast that from four to six years are necessary to train a man for his profession.

The expansion and differentiation of universities into special schools and the large number of students electing professional training have caused the question to be raised as to whether the state can and should continue to pay for this type of training. Should the state force the total cost of training entirely upon the students, it will mean that many of the ablest minds will be denied the privilege of being trained for the various professions. No one would have the temerity to maintain that the best ability is always lodged with those classes that are able to pay the total cost of education. Ability is distributed without reference to the social or economic classes or stations. If life is to be made safe, happiness to be promoted, wealth to be increased, citizenship made more secure, through study for the professions, then every possible means should be taken to attract the ablest minds to the professions, irrespective of the station from which they come.

It is also asserted that the professional schools do

not train enough technicians for the professions, that they are unduly interested in training men for leadership. We may need more mechanics or technicians in the professions, but the day is long since past when we can be satisfied with technicians when exceptionally important questions are being considered. We demand professional engineers, trained lawyers, expert dentists, skilled surgeons. None other will satisfy. If state universities fail to provide such persons, training for leadership in the professions will be left entirely to the privately endowed schools. This should not come to pass. If it does, professional practice within the states will suffer and the science of the professions will be seriously retarded.

The recent growth of state universities has been responsible for another criticism. There are those who fear that too many may be seeking a higher education and that when they have obtained it they will not be willing to do their fair share of the work of the world. This is a result which I do not fear. I believe that the educated person will do his share of the work of the world, and that he will do it better because he has an education. The fact that he has an education will not mean that he will not love to farm, to build houses, to work in the mines, the shops, or the factories. We need more educated persons doing these things.

Furthermore, education offers the only real solution for many of the most acute political and social questions with which we are confronted. Much of the peril of the present situation is due to ignorance. If the universities do not provide sound training on such questions, we may be certain that training will be provided elsewhere. It is not less but more thoroughly sound, impersonal, scientific study of such questions that is needed.

The graduate schools, since their establishment, have been devoted to the advancement of learning. This is dependent upon the ability and initiative of the students. Because they have taken on new functions in recent years, many of the graduate schools have lost the tradition somewhat that they are places for the advancement of learning. For a number of years they have really been schools for the preparation of college teachers. In becoming such they fulfilled a real purpose and responded to a real need, but the advancement of learning for its own sake has suffered in consequence. Graduate students once associated as groups of scholars. They indulged in the free discussion of their common problems and of current questions. But when graduate schools turned their attention to the training of teachers, this common scholarly interest for all graduate students was lost. They ceased to assemble as a body and frequently did not even assemble in groups. Learning for its own sake no longer stimulated them. The only common bond they had was the fact that they were registered in the same school. Instead of becoming scholars in possession of a widely related body of knowledge, they became specialists upon some narrow phase of it. Such persons are not likely ever to become great scholars. The important contributions to knowledge have always been the product of great scholars. Such scholars are not made by students working in small compartments of knowledge. Kindredness of mind, liberalism of spirit, wholesomeness of philosophy result from contact with large fields of integrated knowledge. A tradition of learning we must have. Without it the graduate schools will cease to be a place where learning is loved. Without it science will not advance, learning will disintegrate, and there will be no steadying force in civilization.

Several other forces have contributed to the partial breakdown of the tradition of learning. One has been the advent and growth of the indiscriminate elective system, which happily has now seen its best days. Another cause that has worked to the same end has been the specialization of function in the professions. In place of the general practitioner of medicine we have a specialist upon some part of the human anatomy. Instead of a general course in engineering we have special courses in mechanical, civil, chemical, mining, hydraulic, highway engineering. Business, once a trade, is becoming a profession, with its lines of special service. Every large business establishment now has its expert advertiser, buyer, credit man, sales chief, accountant, and business manager. Every bank has its expert upon insurance, income and profits tax.

All these differentiations are reflected in university administration. Combined with the other forces at work, the university faces the danger of graduating its students with what someone has called "split and partial minds, students whose intellectual attitudes are undisciplined and extemporaneous." It is patent to the student of education that the whole field of knowledge has been divided so frequently for the purpose of creating separate subjects to meet assumed needs that a thoroughly sound education may be denied many students. The splitting of the materials of education into a multiplicity of subjects results in an overemphasis of the materials occurring within a given field, and necessarily leaves the student with a fragmentary conception of nearly every field.

Universities need to make a rigorous study of the materials of education. Nothing would pay larger dividends than for faculties to become students, both of the art of teaching and of the materials of instruction. University teachers are likely to be more interested in discussing administrative measures, financial support, jurisdictional responsibilities, the conservation of their prerogatives, and the programs of their respective professional organizations, than they are in becoming better classroom workers.

When credits and hours and wages and recognition are the main themes of a body of teachers, we may be certain that their idealism has been colored and tinctured by the industrialism of the times, rather than by the professionalism of their calling. Just as many teachers are disposed to emphasize questions and problems that lie at the periphera of their realms, so many students think in terms of numbers of credits and of hours', semesters', and years' work, and the result is that thoroughness of scholarship is in danger of being neglected. If there be any truth or justice in this criticism, it cannot be held to apply with equal force to all units of the university at all times. Wide variation at any given time exists with respect to the completeness with which the various units of the university fulfill their functions. Each unit should inventory its organization periodically and evaluate the results it is obtaining. It should see if it is making its specific contribution to the education of the students in the most effective manner possible.

But even though weakness may exist here and there, the mass results of the university are encouraging. There are certain ideals, there is a certain tone, there is a certain atmosphere characterizing the life of a university that distinguishes it from every other human institution. Whatever these ideals, that tone or atmosphere, may be, it is as truly a function of the university to foster, conserve, safeguard, and stimulate them as it is a function of the university to provide instruction of a specific and definite character. Both make their impacts upon the student. Perhaps the most important of these general functions is the catholicity of spirit the university seeks to inculcate on all occasions. A truly educated man will be, to a certain extent, a cosmopolite. He will be a student of the problems of other nations. He will recognize that his own nation cannot maintain permanently an attitude of singular insularity, for its future is closely knit with that of foreign nations. The loyalty of an educated man to his own country will not blind him to his obligations as a citizen of the world, nor will he be led astray by local and ephemeral interests. The philosophy he cherishes for himself he will wish to extend to the rest of the world.

What is that philosophy? What does the truly educated American believe in? He believes that his institutions are social in origin and in nature, not the product of any individual nor of any group of individuals, that they represent the soul hungers and the spiritual expressions of the common people. He believes that the only natural rights anyone has are those that he uses for collective welfare. He believes in equal rights before the law. He believes in equality of opportunity. He believes that potentially the achievement of the individual is measureless. He believes that a generous education for himself and a better one for his children are the only safeguard of democracy. These are the priceless possession of his creed, the articles of his faith which he desires to have transmitted and made available to mankind everywhere.

It seems strange that it should be necessary to emphasize these truths at this time, when the average man has had his vision widened and his imagination stimulated by the World War. The culture, problems, and interests of other nations are a part of his daily thought. The effect of the individual's consideration of these problems and interests is educational, but the unfortunate truth nevertheless remains that some persons think patriotism means my country against the world, instead of for and with the world. Traditionally we may be narrowly nationalistic, but educationally, economically, and politically this country is a member of the congeries of nations. Our Christian ethics teaches us to be our brother's keeper, and the Golden Rule commands us to do unto others as we would have them do unto us. Any individual who thinks of his job primarily in terms of the money he can earn from it, anyone who thinks of a profession in terms of personal gain, any nation that thinks its problems lie almost entirely within its own boundaries, is on the road to self-destruction. The ancient dividing line between the old world and the new has disappeared. America cannot retain a detached position. The logic of events is demonstrating the utter helplessness and hopelessness of those who cling to such a deluded point of view. Americanism means that we cannot dissociate ourselves from our interests, and our interests require that Europe be lifted out of the mire and restored to life and prosperity.

A university does not engage in propaganda, but its very atmosphere breathes the spirit of helpfulness and of interest in the problems of men everywhere. Its graduates should live in a republic of minds that is not limited by time nor geographical boundaries. If this concept seems ideal it is none the less important for that reason. When a university ceases to be saturated with high-minded cosmopolitanism, a spirit of mutual helpfulness, and a desire to know and to understand the problems of the world, it will cease to be a university. When it gathers under its cloak a spurious cosmopolitanism whose insidious intent is destruction, it becomes a menace to social welfare. This great aim, this fundamental purpose of a true university, we must constantly proclaim from the housetops, that we do not lose sight of it.

Another of the general functions of the university, quite as important as the development of a generous, intelligent, and discriminating spirit of cosmopolitanism, is that of service to the community or state in which the university is located. Perhaps one would say that has always been its purpose and that it has been realized only as universities have sent back to the community or the state efficient graduates. And this statement, of course, is correct. The final measure of value of a university is the kind of service its graduates perform. The university and its graduates underwrite each other. If either declines in merit or worth to the community, the other declines; if either grows stronger and better and serves more nobly, the other improves correspondingly.

There is another way in which a university may serve the community, and that is by assisting it in solving its problems. If the state wishes to know how to beneficiate certain ores, how to eradicate wheat rust, to determine the economic value of peat, to discover the best methods of extracting syrup from cornstalks, how to build roads, how to harness its water, how to eliminate the white pine blister, it will apply to the university for assistance. I foresee a time when state law schools will collaborate with the judiciary in the codification of the laws and in the assembling of legal materials required for the preparation of opinions or decisions. I predict that sooner or later there will be erected, as a part of our engineering schools, institutes of research to which all sorts of practical engineering problems will be brought by the state and by corporations and individuals. It is said that almost

22

a hundred million dollars a year is now spent on engineering problems in private laboratories. The prodigality of this will be recognized eventually and a cooperative arrangement will be entered into with the universities to do much of this work. When this comes true, men of science will not be taken away from institutions of learning, but will be urged to remain there by the very organizations and persons now taking them. I believe that schools of commerce and business will find a corresponding service and that their advanced work will be largely financed by the special projects which they receive from the manufacturing and mercantile establishments of the community.

The principles which will govern the contact of the university with the community will not differ in a single respect from the principles that govern that contact now. The university will refuse to become commercialized. It will not sell itself. It will accept only those projects that have an educational value. It will insist upon the right to publish the results of its researches, and business, whether corporate or individual, will gladly consent to that right.

Every school and college of the university will find larger opportunities for community serviceableness in the future. The school of medicine will enjoy the respect of the medical practitioner. It will bear the same relation as consultant to the practitioner that he bears to another physician. The state will locate general hospitals at the university to which patients will be sent from every section of the state for care and treatment. As health education becomes more universal, community and private hospitals will increase in number. Affiliation between them and the general hospital will be arranged to the advantage of both and to the very great advantage of the people of the state.

There is one other service which the universities should perform and that is the publication of the results of their investigations and researches, particularly those that have a practical bearing upon the everyday problems of the community. Many of these investigations are written in a highly technical language and are filed away for safe-keeping in the archives of the university. They will need to be rewritten in a language suitable for popular consumption and widely distributed to those who may profit by them. There is enough material of this sort filed away in universities to produce important if not radical changes in many fields.

As one contemplates the conception of university education outlined in this paper, he is impressed with its enormous possibilities. He comes to the inevitable conclusion that the great objectives of life will always be reflected in the curricula of the university. Just now these objectives seem to be intelligent citizenship, economic betterment, social and individual justice, and health. Furthermore, the university of the future will be the one best place in all the world for intellectual training, for a mastery of the technique of the professions and the instruments of inquiry and research. It will be a place where men will learn to think in terms of larger units and more abiding forms of service. The state university of the future will never return to the simpler theories and practices of earlier days, yet it will exalt scholarship as truly as it was exalted in those days. The university of tomorrow will have a social vision as well as an effective kind of individualism. It will be dedicated to the making of a better world to live in. It will not neglect its duty as a guardian of the treasury of civilization nor as a pioneer on the frontiers of knowledge, but will acquire a new breadth of interests and sympathies, outlooks, intellectual tastes and appreciations in harmony with the age in which it lives and to which it owes its being.

FREEDOM OF TEACHING

An address delivered on March 9, 1927, before a committee of the Minnesota State Senate

N EARLY three-quarters of a century ago, when Minnesota was inhabited by ten thousand vigorous, adventurous, God-fearing pioneers — in the year 1851 — the territorial assembly adopted a resolution favoring the establishment of a university for the teaching of the arts and sciences. These men had a vision of a great commonwealth ministered to and served by the teachers of the university. Never once in those early years did they seek to limit the work or the activities of the university; never once did they seek to prescribe what it should teach and what it should not teach; never once did they seek to fasten upon it any special creed or doctrine. Unhampered, unrestricted, and unrestrained, they dedicated the university to the teaching of what was known and to the discovery of new knowledge for the benefit of its constituents.

26

FREEDOM OF TEACHING

In your imagination build again the scenes associated with the founding of the university and then turn from them to the one which we have here tonight. Suppose that the shades of those pioneers could return and sit by our sides in this council chamber tonight. With what amazement would they view this assembly and with what consternation would they listen to this discussion! If they could speak, how quickly would they charge us with being recreant to the most fundamental trust ever given to a free people and how quickly would they send us back to study anew the simplest and most elemental lesson of democracy!

The pride in the past which I share with all other citizens moves me so deeply as I contemplate this scene tonight that it is difficult to speak solely and calmly as one you have honored with high responsibilities for nourishing the freedom this bill seeks to strike down. Is it unnatural that I should share with others the amazement they feel when any group seeks legislation on matters which in our American life have been utterly and completely separate from political discussion and action? Is it strange that as a citizen I repudiate what is at bottom an attempt to enforce by law the creed of a group upon the schools of the state? Long ago I learned the simple truth that men cannot be made nor kept religious by law.

And how can I refrain, either as a university administrator or as a citizen, from decrying the use of the police force of the state to fine and terrorize the teachers in the schools and in the university because one group of citizens does not see eye to eye with other citizens? Surely the founders of the state never thought that legislators were expected to accept or reject by law the views of scientists.

I am opposed to this bill for the reason that it is contrary to the genius of American life. The unparalleled progress of American civilization during its brief one hundred and fifty years has been possible because of the freedom of teaching in the schools and colleges. It is true that there have been occasional manifestations of intolerance when the schools have suffered, but always, everywhere, in the long run, the spirit of freedom in speech, in the dissemination of knowledge, and in the pursuit of truth has emerged triumphant. The spirit of America cannot survive in an atmosphere of intolerance or of blind adherence to the doctrines of any group.

The spirit of America will wither and decay when the correctness of scientific theories is decided by legislation or by the counting of heads. If that method had been followed in the past as is proposed today, we should be meeting tonight clothed in the skins of beasts we had killed by bows and arrows. Squatted around a campfire in a cave we should be trying to decide whether to burn or behead some member of our tribe who said that the god of the harvest was greater than the god of the hunt.

By a long upward trail, by trial and error, and after sending to the stake or the rack those who were eager to know the truth and to explain it, the human race has come to cherish learning and to support the labor of scholars. It no longer drags learners before courts and throws men who are seekers of truth into dungeons. It has done wiser and better things. It has founded schools and colleges and universities. In these it has gathered the scholars and thinkers who can find better ways than our fathers knew and teach them to our children. It is to the scientist or the expert in any line that we turn for an answer in scientific matters. We know that he must be free to find the facts as best he may and equally free to seek a theory or hypothesis that explains them. If there is error in his deductions, there is only one way that it can be shown and that is by his own ceaseless and unimpeded search and the labors of his fellow scientists. Mistakes may be made, but unrestricted research is the only means by which they can be corrected. If we are to have better science, we can get it not by legislative decree but by giving teachers and investigators the utmost freedom. If those who know most cannot discover and correct error, we who know less cannot help by majority votes or minority clamor.

I am opposed to this bill for the reason that it will

depreciate the good name and bring ridicule upon the University of Minnesota, not only in neighboring states but in every land from whose native stock we have drawn those who in their day sought freedom from state efforts to enforce dogmas they thought outworn.

From the foundation of the university until our day, the state in the freedom it has given teaching has bestowed upon it an even greater endowment than the supporting funds. In that freedom a great university has been built up. Men have joined its faculty and men have stayed on its faculty because they have found Minnesota freer from hampering influences than many another university.

The labors of these men have brought students from the far corners of the world and honor and profit to the state of Minnesota. It is men such as these, working and teaching in a free atmosphere, that constitute the true glory of the university. It is only because of the state's support of them, not in resources alone but also in the liberty they cherish, that these men have kept and can keep this university in fidelity to the trust imposed upon them. That trust is to represent all, not a few. It is to seek the truth, unshackled by creeds, sects, or parties. We must never forget at the university or in legislative halls that our support comes from men and women of all shades of belief. You and we are the joint trustees on behalf of

FREEDOM OF TEACHING

Christians of many sects, orthodox and heterodox, conservative and liberal, trinitarian and unitarian, of men with religion and of men with no religion. If one group has a right to organize and control the university, then all have; that being true, there will no longer be any university with freedom to serve all and to control its own destiny. When that right is gone, its most priceless possession has been lost. It might lose everything else and still survive; but if this right is lost, its days are numbered. When the scholar who opens the minds of his pupils is called upon to surrender his intellectual integrity, when he is restrained by a statute which prescribes and proscribes what he may and may not teach, then the scholar becomes a hypocrite in the eyes of his pupils and the victim of an intellectual bondage that destroys his sense of self-respect, and civilization enters upon the process of self-destruction. When the spirit of scholarship goes out of a university, the soul of the institution dies. The university will then no longer be a republic of free minds engaged in the high calling of training the youth of a great commonwealth for the exercise of intelligent citizenship.

Do the proponents of this bill suppose for a moment that any salary can draw or keep good men in any department when their freedom and self-respect are taken away from them? I suppose that the men behind this bill think they are striking a blow at one or two departments and a handful of teachers. So far as the university is concerned, they are making insecure our hold upon every good man in the faculty. Many of you may not know directly the departments supposedly liable to criminal action under this bill, but you do know that modern medicine and modern agriculture are based on science and that the men who do our best work in these fields, if not endangered by this preposterous proposal, will be as quick as any to take the first opportunity to escape from the espionage for heresy that is implicit in the bill.

This bill mentions only man, but if the theory about the unchangeableness of man is sound, it should apply, it would seem, equally well to all animal and plant life. If that is so, the doctrines ought to yield a whole flock of bills that would close our stock and plant and fruit breeding experiments for fear they might discover something unpleasant to the advocates of this measure. Then, too, it would seem that the library would require an examination and that thousands of books dealing with the theories of the origin and development of life should be discarded—not books in science alone, but in history, literature, and philosophy. And the youth who attend the university are to have their minds trained and liberalized by avoiding the contamination that would ensue from the dispassionate consideration of the theories of life.

This brings me to the third reason why this bill should not be passed. It should fail because it will not tend to hold more secure the religious faith of our students.

I understand something of the anxiety which an older generation feels concerning the changing ideals of a younger generation. This has always been the case. I can easily see how an active campaign which obscures the real issues could arouse this anxiety to the point of thinking that by law one generation can hold the next to its beliefs of every kind. I can understand this because I belong to that older generation and my life has been spent in association with and service to a newer generation.

The particular kind of anxiety that has been capitalized by those who drafted this bill is the anxiety about the religious life or faith of the next generation. This has led to indiscriminate denunciation of the public schools, the state university, and private colleges founded under denominational auspices. Most of the churches in the neighborhood of the university are actively supported by their faculty membership, and probably as many students are as keenly interested in the religious life as though they were at home. I am not surprised that those who do not know this shout about atheism, which, it is claimed, is being taught by endowed and public-supported institutions alike. The reason is that many do not understand young people and are not willing that their faith shall rest upon their richer knowledge just as the faith of their fathers rested upon a lesser knowledge. We confuse a changing and more significant interpretation of life with a loss of faith when there is no loss of faith.

Such mistaken legislation as is here proposed will only widen the possible differences between the older and the younger generation and increase the disrespect for law which is one of our chief concerns. As for religion, this proposed law can only injure it by its attempt to legislate about matters upon which only experts are entitled to pass an opinion after weighing the available scientific evidence for and against.

The kind of controversy at the basis of this attempt to enact legislation about science is very old. In the two thousand years since the beginning of Christianity, groups of men have arisen from time to time to proclaim that Christian civilization was threatened and Christian faith undermined by teaching that the world was round or that it revolved around the sun, or that there was danger in the wonders discovered by telescope and microscope. Scripture was used by the Greek church to keep many of the Russian peasantry from raising and eating potatoes. The Scotch church once opposed the use of fanning mills for winnowing grain and thought it reason for excommunication because it was contrary to the biblical text that "the wind bloweth where it listeth." These theologians also regarded any farmer using a fanning mill as in league with the devil because he was called in the

Bible "the prince of the powers of the air." In a southern state not long ago a sectarian group opposed the dipping of cattle to make them tick-free on the ground that it was a caricature of the rite of baptism.

Any contention that students will have any sound religious faith permanently destroyed by facing the evidences of science is not borne out by history or by my close observation of students for thirty years.

And why should there be loss of faith when men with scientific training, the great majority of them, bow in humility before His Presence, and with the simplest of faith, a faith founded on reason, worship the God of all? These men of enriched vision and wider knowledge see the handiwork of God in the skies and on the earth round about them. Who dares say that the youth of this generation are being despoiled by these master teachers? Let him learn whereof he speaks before he gives utterance to unbridled condemnation. The spirit of the university is not otherwise than it was in the days of Dr. Folwell and Dr. Northrop.

Though the university and the schools serve all classes of all faiths, the proponents of the bill have gone up and down the state with the proposal that there should be nothing taught not approved by their theology. They have declared that they are going to pass a law, this law, to protect, not Christianity, but their theology; for Christianity, be it always remembered, is the faith alike of evolutionists and anti-evolutionists. But in America these men should be told that the state and church are forever separated. Could there be anything more repugnant to all our American traditions and historic policy than the political philosophy that lurks behind this bill? The sinister consequences of approving it will divide us more than ever into warring camps.

I am opposed to this bill for the reason that I can think of no reasonable justification for it. It will stifle learning, cripple research, destroy intellectual integrity, doom the university to mediocrity or less—and it will not make students more religious. It involves the intrusion of a principle into education, that of passing upon the validity of facts by legislation, that is pernicious in the extreme. It will place the control of the university in the hands of an effective minority. Whenever the control of the university in any form passes into the hands of an outside group or class, its life blood ceases to flow freely and its work and usefulness are retarded. Scholars when they once learn the true inwardness of such a university will shun that university as they would a house with a smallpox sign on it. To pass this bill will be tantamount to serving notice on the scholars of America, if they value their reputation and their peace and happiness, to keep away from Minnesota.

Let us reincarnate the spirit of the fifties and early

seventies of the last century, and let us say to those who seek to destroy that spirit, you shall not crucify the spirit of tolerance, of truth seeking and truth telling, so long as the blood of the pioneers flows in our veins.

Let the doubtful honor of striking a blow at free schools and the principles upon which our government rests pass to such communities and states as do not know how to cherish and defend them.

THE STATE UNIVERSITY : ITS RELATION TO PUBLIC EDUCATION

An address delivered before the Department of Superintendence, National Education Association, on March 1, 1928, in Boston

T HE state universities of America are an expression of the spirit of the pioneers who settled west of the Appalachian Mountains. True, they had their origin in democratic Virginia, but their expansion and development came with the growth of the Central West. Since then they have spread to the South and across the Rocky Mountains to the Pacific Coast.

The state universities represent the culmination of democracy's effort to advance itself by education. They have thrived and flourished where democracy has thrived and flourished. Wholly unsympathetic with every attempt to transplant an alien university system to American soil, the great body of citizens in the Mississippi Valley, and later in the South and West, sought the establishment of institutions of higher learning, open to all, sensitive to public need, supported largely by taxes levied upon all, and designed and administered to promote the public welfare.

The state universities and the public schools evolved out of the same set of conditions. The arguments for the establishment of the universities were essentially the same as those for the establishment of the public schools, only raised to a higher power. The public schools were intended to be free schools; the state universities were intended to be as nearly free as possible. The doors of the public schools were to be wide open; likewise the state universities were expected to admit those who had completed the work of the next lower unit of the public schools. The public schools were maintained to provide for each individual that training by which he could profit most; the state universities offered additional training for those capable of pursuing their studies into still higher realms. Both the public schools and the state universities were founded on the assumption that society's welfare is best promoted by providing as nearly free and equal educational opportunities and privileges as possible. Indeed, from early colonial times this conception has been assumed to be one of the surest guarantees of civil liberty.

But of late a tide of criticism of the public schools in general and of state universities in particular has begun to flow. Today it is a report of one of the great corporations that arraigns the cost of the state universities in most vigorous language and declares that they have become the victims of mediocrity. To-morrow it is a report from one of the great founda-tions declaring that the students should pay the cost of their instruction. The next day it is an address from one of the distinguished citizens of America in which the same declarations are made. Then follows another report, brilliantly written, comparing the best of European secondary schools with American sec-ondary schools of lower grade and discrediting the work of the American schools. Then comes a report from the manufacturers' association calling for new limits on child labor legislation and the extension of the privileges of work for children. Then follows a report of the United States Chamber of Commerce presenting figures showing that education is costing too much. One cannot view an array of statements of this nature without stopping to think. If these criti-cisms and others like them mean anything, they mean that we need to clarify and to redefine our philosophy of life and of education, for it is obvious even to the casual observer or student that a wide difference of opinion exists among the dominant philosophies with regard to education.

The state universities and the public schools from the beginning have been maintained to provide free-dom of opportunity. One of their fundamental doc-trines has been equal opportunity for all to reach their highest attainments. They have stood vigorously against class education. They have provided educational facilities for all alike, the rich and the poor, the boy and the girl, the Gentile and the Jew, the fundamentalist and the modernist, the conformist and the nonconformist, the religionist and the atheist. Free from denominational control, the state universities are nevertheless Christian in spirit, Christian in ideals, and Christian in fellowship.

Long ago they learned that genius and talent do not belong to any class because of wealth or social position. The only differences they recognize are differences due to ability and to a desire to achieve. They recognize that all cannot achieve alike nor move forward at equal rates of speed. They know that some must fall by the way and that some attempt work which they are not qualified to pursue. But they are not willing to condemn those of less talent merely because they have less talent. They propose for them just what they propose for the more talented — that each shall be permitted to progress as rapidly as his abilities will permit to the approximate limits of his attainment. The student of few talents shall not be denied his opportunity while the student of many talents is given his.

The state universities and the public schools have persistently maintained that they are training the common people for the common weal. They have believed in the unlimited potentialities of the individual. In maintaining this as an ideal they have merely been expressing the spirit and philosophy of the free people who support them.

Let the state universities set themselves up as class institutions and the support which they have received hitherto will quickly vanish and out of the soil which gave them birth other institutions will arise to take their places.

All other criticisms notwithstanding, if the American people have any great passion, it is a passion for education. They may not all be imbued with a flair for learning, they may not all be endowed with a "divine afflatus" for truth, but of this one thing we may be certain: no matter how vigorous the criticism of college and university education may be, the people of this country, those who vote and pay the taxes and support its institutions, will not permit their children to be deprived of the privilege of attending college. They will establish new colleges if necessary, even though taxes must be increased to support them.

It is asserted that the average ability of the student bodies in these days is lower than it was fifteen years ago. This may be true; it probably is. But the claim is based upon a priori evidence, and hence is difficult to establish. The standards of admission to college and the standards of college work certainly are higher today than ever before in the history of American education. This is as true of the state universities as it is of the privately endowed universities. If one listens to much of the current criticism he despairs of the college student, but he takes heart when he observes on commencement day that thousands of those who were supposed to be mentally incompetent have completed to the satisfaction of the faculty all the requirements for their degrees. And it should be remembered that these requirements are determined for the most part by those having the alleged superior intelligence of a generation ago.

We hear much about mass education and the absence of the personal touch between university teacher and student. Not all teachers of a generation or so ago held personal communion with their students, either. A few of them did; most of them did not. A student of that day often got very little intelligent advice concerning himself; today he gets advice, scientifically determined, concerning his health, mental make-up, emotional maladjustments, and vocational potentialities.

We probably forget that there were not very many dynamic personalities on the teaching force in earlier days. There were a few, praise be, and most of us acknowledge their strength of character and personal influence. One of the educational myths is that all teachers were of this type. Far from it. We should remind ourselves that there are dynamic personalities who are forceful teachers on the teaching staff today, and that twenty years hence they, too, will be remembered with affection by their students.

Not all state university teachers are of the type which Mr. R. L. Duffus, writing in the Sunday supplement of the *New York Times*, January 8, 1928, describes: "For himself [that is, the teacher in the state university] he needs the arts of the orator quite as much as those of the scholar. He must be ready with stories, with amusing illustrations. He must possess the ability to dramatize his subject, so that the dozing student in the last row will every now and then wake up and grasp a fact or principle." Without claiming that teachers should be entertainers, perhaps a little of the power of lucid presentation may be good for a teacher wherever he is. Experience has clearly demonstrated that men who place themselves rather than the materials of their subjects in the forefront are condemned by faculty and students alike.

In moments of great exultation Americans in general are disposed to praise their schools and the profession of teaching. They view with pride the public schools and the state universities as the agencies of the greatest experiment democracy has ever undertaken. It is the experiment of providing or attempting to provide, largely by taxation, for the education of the children of all men and of offering to them, as nearly free as possible, equal educational privileges from the kindergarten to the university. The burden the present generation has to bear in maintaining this experiment is incomparably lighter than that which our sacrificing forefathers bore to establish this great system of popular education. Certainly it is true that the torch of American civilization has been passed from generation to generation, not by tradition, but through the processes of an expanding education. Will some generation in the comparatively near future witness the dimming of that torch because it provides the maximum opportunity for the children of the favored and denies the maximum opportunity to the children of the less favored?

Americans have long maintained that equality of opportunity is essential to the development, the safety, and the perpetuity of democratic institutions. And none but the most uninformed have ever thought that equality of opportunity meant equality of ability. Equality of opportunity has been relied on to produce a worthy, democratic citizenship.

Education has been supported as a social investment. It has been assumed that society's contribution to the education of its children is returned manyfold in service, progress, and wealth. And the facts, I believe, fully justify that theory. One needs only to point to the states that have neglected education as contrasted with those that provide generously for it, to find evidence in support of this assumption. If one will take the five states that have provided most liberally for education and compare them with the five that have provided most parsimoniously, he will find that the average earnings of the families in the former are almost twice those in the latter, that the amount per individual in the savings banks is nearly ten times greater in the former, that the number of books in the libraries and the number of magazines and newspapers subscribed to is vastly greater, and that the living conditions by and large are much superior.

One of the things we are sometimes prone to forget is that we pay for the things we don't have as truly as we pay for the things we do have, but we pay in a different kind of coin. One has only to sweep his eye over the world to find abundant support for this statement. The nations that have been unwilling to spend on education are the victims of ignorance, superstition, destitution, and of all the wretchedness that comes in their train. America has achieved her station not by a withholding but by a generous spending. And she has done it by refusing to close the gates of educational opportunity. Generous donors and generous states have kept them open. Shall she now turn her back on the past and, heedless of its lessons, initiate a new philosophy, one which provides the best of higher education for the privileged few who possess the money to pay for it? Or shall she continue to hold steadfastly to the theory that democracy in the final analysis is a process of continuous education and that America can keep her place at the forefront among the nations of the world by providing more, not less, generously for the education of all?

If, as most of us believe, society is growing more complex, its problems more numerous, more intricate, and more difficult of solution, then more, not less, education will be required. How tenaciously did our forefathers hold to the doctrine that the progressive advancement of democratic institutions depended upon an educated citizenry! An able attorney said to me recently, "Mr. Coffman, civilization has been ruined by education. Do you suppose you can make people competent to vote on public questions by giving them an education?" My only answer was, "I know of no other way."

And if, as some persons advocate, the education of a generation is to become increasingly selective, so that only the gifted possess knowledge concerning the complex problems of modern life that we are constantly called upon to consider and, we have thought, to assist in solving, if college education is to be only for the select, then it becomes alien to the spirit which gave birth to public education and to the state universities. If pursued to its logical conclusion, this doctrine means that free government, based upon universal citizenship, cannot endure. We are not ready to admit, without adequate trial, that the great American experiment has failed. We are not yet ready to create by deliberate act an uneducated and uninformed proletariat.

We know that there are those who maintain that too many are in school and that too many are being graduated from college. But there does not appear to be any trustworthy information showing that the professions, in general, are overcrowded, and we do not seem to have too many persons with a knowledge of government and of the other institutions of men. Where trained intelligence exists, there we seem to have the best citizenship. And is not citizenship a function which all classes of people are expected to exercise? Shall we deny those who are to traverse the humbler walks of life the outlook of the trained mind? If we attempt to do it we shall probably find ourselves reckoning without our host, for, as Lincoln said, "God must have loved the common people. He made so many of them." And they still rule in the land.

The state universities and the public schools have had still another common interest, an interest to which reference has already been made but which is deserving of further consideration. This interest may be best described by reference to an address which I heard a gentleman deliver recently before a distinguished middlewestern club. He said: "College education, and perhaps secondary education, to some degree at least, should be based upon wealth. Those who are able to pay for it should be privileged to get it; those who cannot pay for it, should be denied it." Here we have a doctrine, stripped of all veneer, that education in its upper reaches should minister only to an aristocracy of wealth.

It is a fact that there are now almost no free universities in this country. The fees charged students by state universities have been increasing, but they are not so large, nor have they increased so rapidly, as fees charged by private universities. If they must now be increased so that the students pay the full cost or approximately the tuition cost of higher education, then one of the original, primary purposes of the state universities will have been defeated.

The gentleman to whom I have just referred declared that all education is simply a matter of charity and that the costs of education should be compared with the money given to charity. Viewed in this way it is clear that education is absorbing an unreasonable proportion of the nation's wealth. He stated also that the disintegrating effects of such charitable giving become even more pronounced in the case of students in colleges and universities, especially if the students are being trained for the more lucrative professions. He demanded that this pauperization should cease because of its deleterious social consequences. It requires a type of reasoning which I am as yet unable to comprehend to understand how those who have themselves been the beneficiaries of this social charity and who because of it have achieved wealth and recognition in their communities should now suddenly discover its harmful effects and seek to deny the children of others and sometimes even their own, the advantages which they themselves enjoyed.

Suppose it should happen that the great privately endowed universities became even more select, that men of means and the great foundations should continue to endow them with increasing millions, and that, at the same time, the state universities were unable to make corresponding progress. Then, indeed, we should have what some claim we already have, provincial education in the private institutions and a cheap variety of education for the less favored thousands in the state institutions. Far be it from me to look with envy upon large gifts to private universities. I am especially happy to see them prosper, but I hold at the same time that the state universities, if the common weal is to be served, should prosper in corresponding degree. Education should be looked upon as a national, not as a local enterprise; as a common, not as a class undertaking.

The country as a whole will flourish best if there are many rather than a few centers where distinguished men of art, of literature, and of science are perpetuating their own kind.

RELATION TO PUBLIC EDUCATION

The last proposition to which I wish to call attention is likewise one to which reference has already been made. Stated more directly, however, the fact is that the state universities and the public schools are unwilling to accept the doctrine of a self-appointed aristocracy of brains as their sole or primary function. They fully understand that there is a somewhat popular impression that wherever "mass" education exists — I deplore the term, for I believe there is no such thing as mass education — but wherever it is said to exist, there is no training for leadership. Yet training for leadership is, in the opinion of many, the only justification for higher institutions of learning. Leadership, it should be remembered, is a relative term. Probably no one is a leader in everything; he leads in some respects and follows in others. Intelligent followership may be quite as important in a democracy as intelligent leadership.

There are those who maintain that the efficiency and value of the higher institutions of learning are determined by the selective and eliminating processes: the fewer they admit and the more they eliminate the better they are. Some, on the other hand, measure their progress by the number of students they attract. Neither of these measures is adequate and neither can be applied without reservation to state institutions. A state institution will eliminate those who cannot do its work, but, if there seems to be good reason for it, it will not refuse to give the individual who can do its work a chance to spend more than four years in accomplishing a given task. It is unwilling to accept slowness as a sure sign of incompetency.

Admission of large numbers of students does not mean that the universities are not training for leadership. They should be offering, if they are not already doing so, every opportunity for the talented and the gifted, and they should be encouraging them in every possible way. In speaking upon this matter, former Dean Eugene Davenport of the University of Illinois said a few years ago: "We hear too much about educating for leadership. What the world wants is not leaders, of whom we have a surfeit, but rather information and trained habits of thinking, that it may select its leaders wisely. This all means the closest possible working relations between the institutions and the citizenship of the state, between those who, feeling the pressure of unsolved problems, realize the need of better information for those whose business it is to supply the need. A university so guided will remain close to the people and close to its problems. A university that so functions will not come very far from fulfilling its highest usefulness."

Two documents dealing pointedly with this general problem have appeared recently. One of them is the January issue of Ginn and Company's leaflet on *What the Colleges Are Doing*, and the other is the annual report of President Butler of Columbia University. The Ginn leaflet is a series of extracts from articles or bulletins which reveal a common theme; they favor rigid selection of students.

Among other things these authors have set up a new conception of social justice. They argue that fewer students should be admitted and more should be eliminated, because the mediocre students are trespassing upon the time and rights of a high-minded faculty who are giving generously and with high altruistic motives of their energy and ability for the advancement of society; because mediocre students are depriving the brilliant students of the opportunity for maximum achievement; and because the mediocre students are defrauding their parents, friends, and society in general of the greater returns and rewards which would accrue if society invested only in the gifted.

The statement is made that "the stampede into college life today is in a great measure blind, ill considered, and without high motive," that the college market is saturated with medocrity, that the keynote of the college world is the tragedy of the unfit, that the colleges are engaged in a wildcat exploitation of youth, that education for democracy should cease, and that education for aristocracy should take its place.

One of the articles in particular seems to hold the colleges responsible for the ills and sins of society.

"For not a third of all that graduate see in their own intellectual growth sufficient compensation for the labors of a college career. Most, on the contrary, feel that they have sacrificed time and energy, and for the loss thus sustained they mean to recover from society. Is the legal profession being prostituted by the practitioner who brings with him into practice the ethics of the bootlegger and the heart of the pawnbroker? Then the remedy is not in stricter requirements for admission to the bar. The evil originates at the threshold of the law school or earlier, and there it is to be combated or abandoned."

I have long known that the schools of this country have their weaknesses but never before did I consider that they should be held primarily responsible for the sins of men. I knew that they had been forced to assume many burdens which did not belong to them, but not until I read these articles did I understand that the colleges of this country, because they have not been exclusive, are responsible for bootlegging lawyers and medical fishmongers. Were this true I should say that it was high time Jehovah directed his destructive thunderbolts at these dens of iniquity.

The common theme running through the series of articles is education for the elect. To this doctrine we agree when it says that those who cannot profit by college training should not be permitted to attempt it or to remain at college. Those who can profit by it but will not, likewise should not be permitted to remain at college. Colleges should not be regarded as playhouses, eleemosynary institutions, or rest stations. At the same time there are those of us who remember with gratitude that talent and genius were not the sole requisites for admission to college in our day.

The authors of these articles say they are thinking in terms of social justice. I maintain that their doctrine is the doctrine of individualism concealed under the cloak of social justice. The conception of social justice advanced by these writers is new in the field of education. While it has been advanced here and there by writers, it never before could be dignified as a movement. Years ago the focus of our attention, educationally speaking, was upon the individual; more recently it has been upon those things which minister to the common welfare. The scene in education has been shifting from man to his activities; from individualism to the common good; from personality to commonality; from what is best for the individual to what is best for the community. And the common good has not been conceived as depending upon the training of the gifted alone, but rather upon the training of all who are competent to profit by it.

In his annual report President Butler distinguishes between universities that reside in the sphere of liberty and universities that reside in the sphere of government. He defines the institutions of liberty as those supported by benefactions, while the institutions of government are those supported by taxes. "Free men," he says, "have themselves erected government and have given to it for domain and occupation a very small part of all that constitutes their activity, physical, intellectual, social, moral, economic, reserving the vast and unlimited remainder for themselves as the sphere of liberty." And again he says, "The vast advantage which a university erected in the sphere of liberty has over a university erected in the sphere of government is in its freedom from bureaucratic control, from partisan political pressure and from those urgings which are the unhappy result of compromise between clashing convictions and conflicting public policies. A university in the sphere of liberty is master of its own destiny and is responsible only to its own ideals and to that larger public which has brought into existence both the sphere of liberty and that of government."

The obvious inference from this is that state universities are greatly limited as to domain and occupation, that is, as to the scope of their usefulness, while endowed universities are practically unlimited as to the scope of their usefulness. If it be true that the social justifications lying back of these two types of universities possess these differences, then it is clear that these two types of universities do not operate and are not expected to operate in the same field. Furthermore, it is clear that we are dealing with differences in kind as well as with differences in degree when we think of the service these two types of universities render. It may be that in the future, even more than in the past, society must rely for its leadership upon the dwellers in the sphere of liberty, while itself providing institutions for the training of citizens for the more modest and humble walks of life. I suspect that if public universities can continue to develop citizens and, if I may dare to say it, "true leaders," as they have in the past, and in increasing numbers, no imaginary line will ever be drawn between a school in the sphere of liberty and a school in the sphere of government.

A second inference to be drawn from Dr. Butler's statement is that endowed universities sustain no interference with their freedom, while state universities do. There is abundant evidence, I believe, in support of the opinion that endowed universities, generally speaking, are influenced, controlled, and frequently governed quite as directly, often more obviously, by the donors of their funds than are state universities by the taxpaying public. The fundamental question of public concern is not that of control versus freedom, for all institutions are controlled; it is the question of whether the control always seeks to advance public interests.

This distinction of President Butler's raises again,

and from a new quarter, the question of the purpose and place of the two types of higher education in a democracy. No matter from what source universities receive their support, they should, in my opinion, seek an atmosphere of freedom in which to do their work, and they should view with disfavor any movement or attempt, whether it be directed at state or at endowed institutions, to curtail their freedom. The subservience of one type must eventually menace the life of the other. A state university, if it is to be worthy of the name, must be as truly a republic of minds where truth is fearlessly sought and taught as is an endowed university. We cannot have two classes of true universities in America, one serving in the empyrean field of liberty and the other with its hands and feet of clay serving in the field of government. Each must serve in both fields if both liberty and government are to survive.

And now in conclusion let me say that both the public schools and the state universities represent the struggles of a free people to establish a system of popular education. The relationship between popular education on the one hand and democratic society on the other is one which the American people still feel with responding devotion. The freer the political institutions of men, the more widely scattered are the schools for everybody; the more restricted the political institutions of men, the less widely scattered are the schools for everybody. The chief means of control in a democracy is some form of popular education. It is no mere accident of time and place that Americans have fostered public education for all. None recognized the truth of this more than Thomas Jefferson, who declared that a free government cannot endure without public education. He gave a mighty impetus to its cause. From then until now the public schools and the state universities have advanced, sometimes with uncertain and halting steps, but in general the movement has always been forward. Could our forefathers have looked into the future, they would have known that this great experiment in democracy was secure, for its foundations are rooted in the idealism of the people and in the provisions which they consider wise for meeting the necessities of their social and political structure.

IV

THE RESPONSIBILITY OF HIGHER INSTITU-
TIONS OF LEARNING FOR THE DEVELOP-
MENT OF EDUCATION

*An address delivered on April 11, 1928, at
the inauguration of Dean William Russell,
Teachers College, Columbia University*

P RACTICALLY all types of higher institutions of learning, privately endowed or tax
supported, have been interested in the development of the public schools, for the reason that
the colleges and universities have depended largely
upon the public schools for their students. The articulation of the privately endowed institutions with
the public schools has been less intimate than that of
the state universities. In the early days the endowed institutions frequently admitted students with no training other than that received at home or by tutors. In
more recent years they have maintained a system of
entrance examinations, or some other type of selective
device, while the state universities, because they have
considered themselves as parts of the general scheme
of public education, have maintained wide open doors
for all the graduates of the public schools who wished
to attempt a higher education.

RESPONSIBILITY FOR EDUCATION

The fact that the colleges and universities have occupied what they have been pleased to call the higher realms of education has, in not a few cases, produced an air of superiority and aloofness in their relation to the "lower" schools. And that feeling, I fear, has not entirely disappeared from their ranks. Indeed, there is considerable evidence that it is increasing in some quarters, for the criticism of the public schools is active, severe, and voluminous. The claim is made that they are poorly organized and poorly taught, that they are diffusive rather than thorough, wasteful rather than efficient, and withal incompetent for the task they are supposed to perform. These criticisms come pretty largely from those who reside in these "higher spheres" of thought. In some instances, certainly, they offer stones when bread is needed. It is not sufficient for one to seek the higher altitudes of purified thought and there purge his mind of responsibility for a situation which he or his institution has aided in creating. Responsibility cannot be shed simply by absolving oneself from it.

Fortunately we are living in an age in which we promptly ask for evidence, for facts to support contentions. We ask for them in this case. We want the facts about the schools. The colleges have trained teachers for them, written textbooks for them, advised them concerning their curricula, their modes of discipline, their forms of organization, and their

61

administrative procedures, and in many other ways sought to improve them. Harsh criticism by the colleges now must reflect back upon themselves.

But colleges missed the mark when they looked upon the public schools merely as preparatory to college. At that point diverging philosophies came into conflict: one represented by public opinion and the other represented by university opinion. The public recognized the school as an agent of the community and the state, while the college thought of it as a lower and subordinate institution. The public supported the school in the interest of the common welfare, the college thought of it as a feeder to itself. While the colleges were writing textbooks and training teachers, the public lengthened the school year and introduced all sorts of subjects designed to train students vocationally and to instruct them in matters of health and in civic and social responsibilities. While the colleges were attempting to mold the schools according to comparatively static and traditional programs, the public schools dared to break with tradition, to try out new methods, to "psychologize" materials. While the colleges imposed formal requirements, prescribed units, and "logical" procedures, American education became public education in a real sense. It refused to acknowledge the dominion of the college. Democratic in origin and in purpose, quickly responsive to public need, essentially progressive in nature, it sought to serve the free people who created and who maintain it. It now accepts the philosophy, inherent in American thought, that the safety and progressive development of the fundamental institutions of democratic America depend upon a high level of trained intelligence among all the people and that each individual is entitled to educational opportunity in keeping with his ability and power of achievement.

The college by reason of its exclusiveness and isolation has not responded so readily to social need as has the public school. Medieval in origin and essentially conservative in nature, it has been slow to change. It modifies its practices slowly and frequently only under pressure.

It is obvious that there is virtue in both these points of view. Each serves as a check upon the other. The pathway of progress lies between; it is uneven and irregular, sometimes difficult to discern, at other times broad and conspicuous. In searching for that pathway let us remember that the college is not wholly conservative, nor the public school wholly progressive. I am talking in terms of emphasis rather than in terms of inclusiveness.

Democratic society has insisted on the school offering training along many lines, and it has provided the funds for it. Each succeeding lower economic level of society demanded for its children the educational privileges possessed by the children of the higher economic levels. With the extension of the right of suffrage there was a corresponding extension and expansion of public education. In other words, public education became universal because the people insisted upon equal educational rights for all and special privileges for none. Right or wrong, that is the dominant American philosophy with regard to education. We have staked the future of our country upon it. And we still believe in it.

Of course, there could have been only one outcome of such a philosophy, and that was to draw more students. Soon vast numbers, in inclination and training quite unlike those who had been in college a generation before, were clamoring at the doors of the higher institutions of learning. At first they were welcomed, and the college authorities pointed to the increased registration as a measure of their success. Later and more recently they have looked upon these larger numbers as a menace and have sought by numerous devices to prevent them from entering or to dismiss them soon thereafter. The immediate effect of this new policy has been to raise into relief again, and with added emphasis, the whole question of the purpose of American education. Higher education has been responsible for raising the issue, and in my judgment must be responsible for an answer to it which will satisfy American public opinion.

It is a matter of common knowledge that the public schools have been venturesome; they have not been content to follow blindly the leadership of the colleges. They have dared to think for themselves and to initiate their own programs. They have dared to expand and to modify their programs even though the expansion and the modification did not conform to the requirements handed down from above. This independence of thought and of action has been a great source of strength to them in their local communities, but it has widened the gap between them and the colleges rather than increased articulation with the colleges. The public schools have been unwilling to measure their achievements wholly in terms of so many units of something or other. They have set up programs adjusted to the aptitudes and choices of the students, particularly in the field of secondary education. They have not measured their success by the number they have excluded but rather by the number they have directed into useful channels.

It would be the sheerest folly to maintain that the public schools have been wholly right and the universities wholly wrong, or that the universities have been entirely right and the public schools entirely wrong with respect to this development. The truth must lie somewhere between. It is obvious that both these types of institution will continue to exist and that some cooperation between them is inevitable. As has already been intimated, the practical question is what shall be the nature of this cooperation and how can it be made as effective as possible?

To increase the effectiveness of this relationship one thing clearly must be recognized, and that is that neither the public schools nor the universities can maintain a detached point of view toward the other. Both must recognize their common function and both must appreciate the fact that the old order changeth, that the schools of yesterday do not fit one for today and that the schools of today will not train for tomorrow. The colleges and universities must recognize and appraise more highly than they do at present the public service function of the public schools, and the public schools must with equal fairness recognize the importance of training the talented and the gifted for the higher fields of service.

The arguments favoring the establishment and the maintenance of the public schools are as potent today as they ever were, but the conditions of life for which the schools are supposed to train are being transformed by forces so silent and yet so powerful in nature that we are scarcely conscious of what is actually taking place.

The older generation knows that the education which served it will not serve today. It knows that life is swifter, that its contacts are made over wider areas, that competition is keener and severer, and that the problems of politics, of commerce, of business, of education, of religion are increasing in number and in difficulty. It surveys the social horizon not so much for an explanation of the swift-moving currents of changing life as for a solution of the problems which they create. In searching for remedies, however, it is necessary to look for causes.

A generation ago life was relatively simple and its problems easy of solution. Now it is complex and its problems difficult of solution. Then a simple curriculum of reading, writing, and arithmetic sufficed; now a complex one is required. Then there were a few "thought" or "reflective" subjects; now the presence of many "expressive" subjects constitutes one of the tests of the schools' socializing period. Then method was based upon trial and error, now upon science. Changes in the schools are the laggard indications of a changing social order. And how seldom do we pause to note that the spirit of the schools is but a reflection of the *Zeitgeist* of the period. How rarely do we pause and take stock of the changes that are occurring in the social order round about us. And yet it is only by noting these that we can comprehend the problems and the philosophy of American education. Perhaps a hasty glance at some of these changes may help to clarify our thinking.

Less than forty years ago the lad residing in the country village still had ample opportunity for the exercise of initiative; now that opportunity is gone,

for all across the prairies the small towns are vanishing like ghosts in the night. In the place of the country store there has come the chain store; in the place
of the country doctor there is now the specialist who
resides in the city. The bank is tributary to a great
system of banks which reaches into one or more of
the great economic centers of the country. Even the
creamery is a part of a corporation which extends into
remote parts of the country. The people who reside
in the community no longer trade there exclusively.
With good roads and the automobile available, they
think nothing of driving to the city, fifty or a hundred
miles away, to do their shopping. There is little or
nothing left of the old town; youth will not stay
there; the spirit which made it is dead or dying; the
inventiveness of the generations that built the community is vanishing with its builders; the young people
born and bred there have lost much of the power of
self-entertainment; something seems to be passing out
of the life of America, and that something is a thing
that did much to make America.

What are we substituting for the initiative and independence of the individual, which were so stimulated by the local pride of the community? We are
substituting a long-term apprenticeship in business,
not for all, but for thousands and thousands of the
young people of today. The youth finds it is more
and more difficult to establish a business of his own,

the success of which depends upon his own enterprise and initiative. Now he finds it necessary to secure employment in the great mercantile or manufacturing establishments, or in a public service corporation, or a chain store, or some other institution of a highly organized and diversified character. The duties of his first position are simple in character, but he soon finds that someone has been there ahead of him and that all the experiences it is possible for him to have, this person has had and recorded. He is expected to do the work in accordance with the written or printed instructions and to file his reports as the prescriptions indicate. When he has become sufficiently habituated to the routine of the position, he is advanced to another position which is more difficult than the preceding one, but in which the work, like that in the first, is essentially routine in character. Step by step, usually through long years of experience, the youth advances from one stage to another, becoming more and more highly trained and more and more proficient in the routine performance of his work. He is not expected to make mistakes and to profit by them as the youth of a generation ago did. He is expected to acquire perfection, to do as he is told to do in the way in which the prescriptions indicate; he checks in by the clock and he checks out by the clock. When one remembers that this youth is typical of tens and hundreds of thousands of others, he cannot help reflecting on what this type of life must mean eventually for our social order. It means that thousands are acquiring docility of mind where once there was mental alertness born of initiative and independence.

The controlling motive of these great organizations is the payment of dividends. The individual who works for them all too frequently bears an impersonal relation to those in control, for they are far removed from him. He is not known to them by name, nor as an individual, but the statistics of his office are checked at regular intervals for the purpose of determining whether the net revenue is holding its own or is increasing. All this is done in the name of the modern god before whom we bow — the god of efficiency.

This industrialization of business has invaded practically every phase of human life. One observes it entering the practice of medicine, for more doctors rather than fewer are being placed on salaries; one finds it entering the field of law, for great corporations of law, consisting of many employees, are coming into existence here and there; one even finds it entering the field of agriculture, where large-scale farming by tenants who are employees is being advocated; one finds it everywhere.

While these great corporations and organizations are growing fat and their power and influence are increasing, what is happening to those who are in their employ? One thing seems certain: we are in considerable danger of developing a clerical type of mind which will have less and less interest in personal improvement, less and less concern about the business in which it is engaged, which thinks more about a day's work as calling for so much salary than about a day's work as affording so much opportunity for advancement and growth. With the increasing tendency of corporations to desire training to fit individuals into occupational niches, thus closing the road to promotion to them, one cannot avoid the fear that we are facing the prospect of a docile and unthinking proletariat.

It must be obvious, of course, that this generation will not give up the products of science, that it will not relinquish the conveniences that science has brought into the household and into all the fields that minister to its comfort; so that now we face the dilemma of trying to preserve something of the initiative which built America and at the same time something of that efficiency which has increased our resources and our comforts and conveniences.

We know that life is being transformed before our very eyes. We profit by it, but we do not understand it, and there is no social philosopher to point the way out. The slow-moving columns of humanity march to the step of science and industry without knowing where such leadership is taking them. New inventions and increased business are praised on every

71

hand because they mean more wealth. Apparently no one is willing to accept the assumption that science may develop to such a point that society may become the victim of its own achievements. And yet we are faced on every hand with increased unemployment due to the introduction of new and improved machinery. One machine now does the work of many men. It is so in every trade and industry, even agriculture. How those who are driven out of work, and often skilled work, too, because of the introduction of machines, are to be absorbed in productive work, is still an unsolved problem. Hitherto we have trusted to chance and Providence to provide; now it appears that we must assume some responsibility for the situation ourselves. Surely higher education must help to find the way, and the public schools must do much to train our people to follow the way when it is found. No greater problem than this is likely to arise to challenge the educational statesmanship of our times.

Thus far I have confined my attention to sketching changes occurring in the industrial world. These affect largely intellectual development. Changes in other aspects of life are quite as fundamental and as far reaching in their significance. Take morals for example. The battle cries of conscience which thrilled us a generation ago are no longer sufficient. Old forms of security can no longer be trusted. Fresh social parasites have been let in upon us. New social puritans must be born and trained to solve the problems of this age.

We have long known that new civic standards are required. The evidences of a lack of civic responsibility are to be found on every hand. The most obvious evidence is found in the fact that in this presumably enlightened country only about 50 per cent of the voters express their judgment even at presidential elections. In spite of the fact that the American schools, the greatest experiment in democracy the world has even seen, have been providing education for practically all the youth of the country for nearly two generations, we are ignorant and uninformed on political matters and slothful in the discharge of our duties as citizens. The American vice is that of letting other people, particularly those working in the fields of politics and morals, do our work for us, while we sit around and complain about the manner in which they do it. This circle of indifference works havoc with the public mind. We have become hardened toward corruption in public life or we have settled into a conscious state of helplessness. When it is exposed we are caught in a tidal wave of condemnation, but the wave is purely emotional. It seldom makes a difference in our conduct. We cry out with vigor against paternalism in government only to accept it with equanimity if it seems to serve our special interests. We inveigh against fanatical attempts to enact into mandatory law group prejudices, only to accept such legislation if it serves our particular ends. When sovietism invades legislative halls we hold up our hands in consternation, only to accept it when it ministers to our class. We may evade all these responsibilities, but we do so at the price of losing some of our most precious legacies.

There are those who say that there were never so many deflections from rectitude, so much positive immorality and criminality, as today. They then use this as an indictment of youth and of education. If the schools are debasing a generation in ethical ideals and moral conduct, they should be destroyed. But what are the facts? Are the schools making these troublesome social situations, or are they merely trying to cope with them? Clearly the world of today is different from that of thirty or forty years ago. Then we had no automobiles, no wireless, no moving pictures, no aeroplanes, no radio, few electrical appliances. The eight-hour labor law was not general, and it was practically unheard of for women. There was no woman's suffrage and women's clubs were few. Music had not been invaded by jazz, and the literature and drama of the day were not devoted to sex exploitation.

Mrs. Susan Dorsey, superintendent of the Los Angeles schools, a woman of penetrating judgment, writing upon this very matter says, "For the most part, it was a clean-hearted America, troubled greatly about the saloon and the liquor traffic, and exceedingly anxious about every source of moral contamination to youth; it was waging battle royal against certain questionable pictures enclosed in packages of cigarettes and objectionable depictions of the feminine form on billboards; a world in which woman's dress was hideous, I grant you, but sufficient; and withal, a world which held strictly to standards of reserve in feminine matters."

America today is nothing like that. The problems of character training are as different from those of forty years ago as night from day. As Mrs. Dorsey says, "All through the movies, the drama, fiction, and magazines, we find little of that interpretation of those human emotions which have at all times nerved the hearts and steadied the hands of men and women to deeds of courage or heroism, which have found expression in acts of justice and mercy, those emotions which are embodied in the noblest works of art and the greatest institutions of human society — alas, much of our art and literature seems to have lost its cunning and, instead of live coals of clean-hearted human life and aspirations, it offers youth the burnt-out embers of sensuality and passion."

The fault is not with the youth of our generation; the fault is with the times. Our mode of life is essentially insurgent, centrifugal, and romantic. There can be no doubt that many of the ideals, standards of action, and forms of procedure which our clear-sighted forefathers advocated as a measure of safety for the nation have grown dim. We are faced with a summons to clear thinking and self-discipline such as we never experienced before.

The practical question which we do not propose to lose sight of wholly in this discussion is, What bearing do these changes have upon the responsibility of higher institutions of learning for the development of American education? We are not yet quite certain of the answer to that question, although it is becoming reasonably clear. Certain things are happening which will help to make it still clearer. One of these things is the great influx of students into the public schools and into the higher institutions of learning. In the last analysis this is due, in my opinion, largely to the consequences of expanding machinery, loss of employment for thousands, the closing of many small business concerns, the absorption of many in the great corporations, the spread of the chain store, the decadence of many local communities, the standardization of the industrial output. The older generation, observing these changes and not knowing what to do, has sent its children to school in increasing thousands, hoping thus to provide for them preparation to face this changing order. Under these circumstances our responsibility becomes quite clear.

The majority of the students in colleges are not

there because they expect to become great leaders. They are there because they hope to be trained for something useful in life. This sets the college its major task. If the colleges fail to provide them with such training, other types of schools will be established that will do so.

American society wishes to maintain a certain standard of living — the present one at least and a better one if possible; it wishes to enjoy the fruits of science and of organized industry; it wishes to preserve opportunity for initiative in fair measure; and it is looking to education to point the way out.

American society will not be satisfied with the reconcilement of the conflict between opportunity and efficiency; it desires a program of education consonant with the social and political problems of the times; it demands a new set of moral values and an acceptance of moral responsibility. It declares that in a constitutional and representative government safety lies in the character of its citizens, in their willingness to accept responsibility as well as in their trained intelligence and occupational opportunities. The great ethical values of the race, its great social inheritances, are found not in wealth, in efficient industrial organization, in well distributed opportunity, or in political liberty, but in spiritual relationships which should guide us in ways of tolerance and good will.

It is my candid opinion that the time has now come

when the higher institutions of learning of this country need to assume a new responsibility for the development of American education. Up to the present time they have concerned themselves with training teachers and with all sorts of research relating to the public schools. These functions are necessary and must be continued. But the heaviest responsibility which these institutions face is that of interpreting the changing forces of life. This interpretation obviously will call for a modified point of view and a progressive program of education. It will call for a program which will serve on the one hand as an antidote for the industrialization of life and which will on the other hand give the student, according to his capacities, such training as will enable him to achieve a reasonable measure of success in the industrial order. It will call for a program which trains one to be cosmopolitan and catholic in his point of view. It will call for a program which emphasizes sacrifice, renunciation, duty rather than pleasure, satisfaction, and self-gratification, and it will call upon all the agencies of life to work to this end.

In other words, the great responsibility resting on our institutions of higher education is that of assisting the American people to understand the shifting currents of the times and to organize an educational program which will best serve humanity, both young and old, in the light of these changes. The gravest responsibility of higher education is not that of determining how much a building costs, how many years of training a teacher needs, or how rapidly the children should progress; it is understanding life, and in the light of that understanding, organizing a curriculum which will orient the students into that life and train them to be citizens as well as workers in a republic. In other words, the responsibility of higher institutions for American education is what it has always been: it is the responsibility of joining with the public schools in defining the philosophy of living in these modern times and of reinterpreting and readjusting the program of education for the masses in harmony with it.

V

THE RELATION OF THE UNIVERSITY TO THE STATE

State Day Convocation address delivered at the University of Minnesota on December 6, 1928

I REGARD it as one of the hopeful signs of the times that the students have insisted upon having a part in the exercises of this day. There is no good reason why they should not assume greater responsibility, and even the initiative — in cooperation with the university administration, to be sure — in arranging for the annual exercises of State Day. Upon this occasion it is right and proper that everyone interested in the welfare of the university and of the state should take a careful inventory of the relationships existing between these two institutions, and upon none should a heavier responsibility fall in this regard than upon the students of the university, who must soon bear the burdens of citizenship.

The history of the University of Minnesota reaches back to early territorial days. The university pursued a more or less uncertain and uncharted course from

1851 until 1869, when Dr. Folwell became president
of the institution. His inaugural address is one of the
most significant pronouncements on higher education
ever delivered in America. Among other principles
which he emphasized in this address none is more
significant or more profound than the following: "I
am content merely to urge that university education is
essential to the *well-being* rather than to the *being* of
the state." It is quite obvious that a state can exist without a university. A state may exist without research,
without educating its leaders, without educating its
common people, and without the wealth, the conveniences, and the blessings which follow in the train
of education; but a state that desires these things and
desires them in increasing abundance will spend increasing amounts upon education. Indeed, such a
state will look to the future and attempt to make provision for growth beyond any given generation, and
it will likewise attempt to make provision for the
continued development of its university; for it will
recognize that the university is, as Dr. Folwell said,
"essential to the well-being rather than to the being
of the state."

Dr. Folwell recognized the importance of planning
for the future. He even urged that the state provide
some form of liberal endowment for the university.
This idea was not new, for the same suggestion was
made in 1851, when there existed a population of only

about ten thousand people in the territory. The federal government undertook to provide an endowment for the university when it set aside federal lands for its maintenance, and the state of Minnesota has attempted to do so since then on several occasions. But not all these forms of endowment have created a fund large enough to take the university out of the sphere where, of necessity, its financial needs are treated as if they were those of a department of the state's political mechanism.

The endowment efforts of the federal and state governments have not been large enough to insure the university an easy and natural growth and development. This is a matter deserving of the most thoughtful consideration on the part of the people of the state. If the University of Minnesota could have assigned to it an endowment fund with as much money as will be spent on highways in this state during the next five years, it would produce an income equal to the amount which the state will be called upon to appropriate annually for the support of the university. Such a plan would enable the state to reduce its annual appropriations for the university to the point where large sums would be available for other constructive works desired by the taxpayers of the state.

It should not be understood that I am advocating that the state use the highway fund to provide an endowment for the university. I am too enthusiastic a supporter of good highways to be guilty of this indiscretion. I believe that a people that can find the funds to build highways can likewise find the means to support higher education in all its forms. I remember that Rome built her Appian highway but perished miserably because she failed to give corresponding attention to the sciences and the humanities.

In the early days those sturdy pioneers who were responsible for the founding of the university held tenaciously to certain principles:

First, they insisted that the University of Minnesota should be a democratic university with regard to what should be taught. They made provision for instruction in agriculture, in medicine, in the theory of teaching, and in the various arts and sciences.

Second, they insisted that the university should be open to all and that it should be under the control of no sect, no group, no organization. They seemed to recognize that if it lost its freedom to direct its own destiny it lost its most priceless possession.

And finally, they declared that it should be as nearly free from fees as possible, and they even went so far as to suggest the possible hope that all fees should be abandoned. Now we find a widespread argument that students should be required to pay the full cost of their education and that higher education should be made available only to those who can pay for it.

THE STATE UNIVERSITY

There are two radically opposed points of view prevailing today with regard to the function of a state university. One of these is represented by those who insist that state institutions should train leaders, that they should admit only the gifted students, the elect. The advocates of this doctrine insist upon rigid entrance requirements; they do not shed any tears over heavy student mortality; they are training an "intellectual aristocracy." The psychological effect of this doctrine upon those who attend and succeed in college is no graver, in my opinion, than the reflex psychological effect of this doctrine upon the faculty.

The other point of view with regard to the function of a state university is that its activities will not be confined to the training of those who are to exercise leadership, but that a responsibility rests upon it to serve the entire state in whatever way the facilities of a great teaching and research center can be effectively used by the largest possible number of citizens of that state. According to this point of view it will be clearly recognized that not all those who practice law will be great lawyers; that not all those who practice medicine will be great doctors or great surgeons; nor will all those who graduate from schools of business be great financiers. Leadership is thus recognized as a relative matter. No one leads in all respects; each follows part of the time, in fact most of the time.

84

And again, according to this point of view, a state university is serving the legal profession when it is turning out better and better lawyers, the medical profession when it is turning out better and better doctors and surgeons, the business world when it is turning out better bankers, merchants, manufacturers; and in turning out better lawyers, and doctors, and bankers — better trained minds — it is serving the interests of the state.

It is perfectly clear that these two points of view are in constant conflict. Those who founded the state university were disposed to emphasize the second. In these latter days there is a not inconsiderable element of our population that urges the former. It makes an enormous difference which of these two philosophies shall prevail; in other words, which shall control our policies. It is highly important that the people of the state and the students themselves shall give careful consideration to this matter.

It is certainly true that there is a considerable portion of the population that believes the university was established and is maintained to accomplish or achieve some social program. They think, for example, that the broad purpose of the medical school is to provide the community with an adequate and continuing supply of learned and skillful physicians, that the broad purpose of the law school is to provide the community with an adequate supply of learned and skillful lawyers, and so on throughout the entire list of professions and vocations for which the university may provide training.

In contrast to the opinion that the university is maintained to accomplish some social purpose and to provide a quota of trained professional leaders in various fields, there is the personal point of view that is represented by the parent who has a son or a daughter at the institution. The parent is not always willing to subscribe to the view that society maintains these institutions of learning for the purpose of providing a limited number of trained persons in each of the scholarly and professional fields. The parent still feels that his individual rights have not been and should not be submerged entirely in a more or less abstract social program.

Not long ago a mother telephoned me from a distant section of the state, saying that she wished to see me at my office on the following day but that she did not desire to have her son know that she was making this call. When she came she told me that she was a dressmaker and that she had assisted her son through high school, that he had worked a year, saving his money that he might come to the university, and that he was not starting off well in his college work. She clearly had the feeling that society is maintaining the university largely for the benefit of her son. She knew well that he did not possess the natural qualities of leadership, yet she believed that if he could have ample time to re-establish habits of study he would do satisfactory work at the university.

Within a week I received a communication from a father who lives in a distant section of the state saying that he wished to call on me some evening and that he did not desire to have his son know he was making this call. He, too, was interested in inquiring about the progress of his son. If I had said to him that the state of Minnesota was maintaining the law school for the purpose of turning out a limited number of highly trained lawyers and that his son did not possess the natural qualifications to measure up to this high standard of excellence, he would have been offended. What he asked for was a fair chance and a square deal for his son; no more. He believes that his son possesses sufficient ability to do thoroughly satisfactory work, and he seems to be justified in that opinion.

One needs to remember that with more than eleven thousand students in the university there are, at any one time, twenty thousand or more parents who have a deep personal interest in the welfare of these students and who look upon the university as their one great opportunity to provide additional training and an enlarged prospect for their children. The sacrifices they have been making and are still disposed to make are not in the interest of some abstract idea or some abstract program, but for the benefit of their children.

THE STATE UNIVERSITY

Now this brings me to a consideration of the kinds of students we have at the university. A recent book, *College or Kindergarten,* by Dr. Charles Maxwell McConn of Lehigh University, says there are three classes of college students. The "bread and butter" students are those who wish to take vocational or professional training for the purpose of earning more money. The "super-kindergarteners" are those who have ample funds to pay any reasonable tuition fee and who are not greatly interested in improving their minds. Dr. McConn suggests that this group of students should have a separate college built somewhere out in the country. It should have Gothic buildings, stained glass windows, ivy on the walls, long avenues with beautiful trees arching over them. It should have its stadium and all the extracurricular activities. Such fees should be charged as would enable the institution to operate without calling upon outside sources for funds. No student should be sent home during his entire four years of college except for gross immorality. The third type of student to which Dr. McConn calls attention is a small group consisting of those who are interested in ideas, in thinking, in acquiring information, in learning for its own sake.

Now the University of Minnesota, like every other higher institution of learning in America, has all three types of students. Since they are probably all here this morning I wish to lay especial emphasis upon the

fact that young people in college today, and particularly in the state universities, have an obligation as
well as an opportunity. I agree with President Little
of Michigan, who declared recently that every student in a public institution is in a certain sense a paid
servant of the community. If the public engages a
contractor to construct roads for it, paying for the
roads out of the taxpayers' money, it expects the contractor and all his crew to work hard and honestly
and to put in all the quality of material as specified by
contract. The same thing is true in public education.

Education is not a game; it is a contract. It is therefore quite proper to ask the questions: Why should
students do less than they can? Why should they be
allowed to do less than they can? Why should they
be allowed to put in an inferior brand of construction
at public expense? When the public deals with public
employees it throws out those who waste time. There
are undoubtedly some social justifications for this in
the case of college students. We do not allow men
to build a public building unless we know perfectly
well what they are doing. Suppose a contractor is
caught cheating at a piece of state construction, what
happens to him? Suppose there is a student caught
cheating in his class work. If the analogy is carried
through, what should happen to him? It must be perfectly clear that colleges cannot create ability, nor do
they look upon opportunity as equivalent to achieve-

ment. On the other hand, it is the business of those who enjoy the benefits of colleges to utilize their ability to the utmost and to take every honest advantage of their opportunities in order that they may compensate society in part for what it has invested in them.

Of course the other side of this picture is found among those who are disposed to admit all comers and then fail them in cold-blooded style simply for the sake of getting rid of them. Recently I received a letter outlining the policy of another university with regard to the admission and elimination of students. It stated that this institution, because it is a state institution, admits all high school graduates without question but that it has adopted a deliberate policy of failing them by the hundreds for the purpose of eliminating large numbers. This to my mind is little short of criminal. It indicates a woeful lack of responsibility and a complete disregard of the obligations of the institution to the vast number of students.

This discussion, of course, is necessarily somewhat discursive. But it would not be proper, it would seem, for me to close the discussion without asking the question, What benefits does the state expect from those who have enjoyed its bounties at the university? Without going into details, it seems to me that the state has a right to expect that those who have attended the university will be more productive than those who have not. If they became lazier and less productive than those who have not enjoyed corresponding advantages, one of the social justifications of the existence of the university would be destroyed.

A second benefit which should accrue from a college education is that of a more enlightened citizenship. College-trained men and women should be disposed to consider every question open-mindedly and on its merits and to decide its issues in terms of public good. They should be the evangels of creative Americanism.

Third, college men and women should improve the intellectual standards of living. No matter in what walk of life they may move and have their being, whether it be that of high and distinctive leadership or of a humbler character, the training they have received should result in higher and more intellectual standards of living.

Fourth, those who have enjoyed the benefit of college training should be tolerant, catholic, considerate of the opinion of others. It is necessary that especial attention be paid to this even in these days, for with three hundred years of college training in America, it does not appear that a generation of tolerant college graduates has been produced. The issues of life are still being decided entirely too frequently on the basis of bias and prejudice.

Fifth, college men and women should be honorable

in their dealings with others — not like that young law student who said that he was studying law in order to learn how to evade the law.

Sixth, college graduates and former students should have a social point of view. They should not think of their professions primarily in terms of money-earning power and of prestige, but of their social value. A law graduate, for example, should think more of further-ing the cause of human justice than of the size of his fee, a medical graduate give more consideration to the cure of human diseases and the discovery of new cures than to personal prestige. The only possible way for civilization to make progress is for those who have enjoyed its privileges to exhibit in their daily walks and in communion with each other a highly social point of view.

And finally, college graduates should stand for the progressive advancement of learning. The goal they set for themselves should be a goal which can never be realized; it's one which lies just ahead; it's one which calls continually for more effort; it's one which stimu-lates the search for truth and calls for more knowl-edge in every field of human welfare.

In summing up I should say that the state expects the college graduates to be more productive, better citizens, to improve the intellectual standards of liv-ing, to be catholic and tolerant of the opinions of others, considerate, honorable in their dealings with others, to have a highly developed social point of view, and to stand for the progressive advancement of human learning.

It should be remembered that the significance of a college lies not in what the students bring to it but in what they take away, and that the measure of success of a college is not the number of persons who receive diplomas on commencement day but the kind of lives those persons live a generation after the diplomas have been handed to them.

VI

THE UNIVERSITY AND THE MODERN WORLD

An address delivered on November 21, 1929, at the inauguration of President Raymond A. Kent, University of Louisville, November 21, 1929

UNIVERSITIES have been compared to lighthouses, whose light radiating in all directions dispels darkness, giving hope to the weary mariner and making it possible for him to find his way home. They have been likened to dynamos at some great central station whose power lines reach into every section of the community, giving strength and renewing life and energy. Recently they have been referred to as factories more interested in quantity than in quality, more concerned about numbers than about personality.

All these comparisons are mere figures of speech. Each chooses certain similar qualities to emphasize: hope, promise, encouragement, in the case of the lighthouse; power, strength, energy, in the case of the dynamo; numbers, quantity, output, in the case of the factory.

A university consists of something more than a

single set of factors. By its very name, as well as by its very nature, it is universal in purpose and in scope. It sheds light, it develops new power, and it transmits knowledge. But the light it radiates, the power it develops, and the knowledge it transmits do not remain fixed and unchanging generation after generation. The lighthouses must be built taller, the dynamos made more powerful, and knowledge must be disseminated over wider and wider areas, if progress is to be made.

Universities are social agencies which the people create and maintain to promote their welfare and to advance civilization. Unless their very atmosphere is surcharged with the spirit of unrest and intellectual dissatisfaction, they soon become hoary objects of tradition and reverence rather than instruments of progress. They do not come into existence, nor are they maintained, merely because people wish to preserve the past. They are not museums for preserving culture — although the maintenance of institutions for this purpose is not unworthy; rather, they come into existence to train successive generations of youth for the work of a new day.

Only the spirit remains generation after generation; the form constantly changes. The very subjects which are necessary for a liberal education change from period to period and from century to century. Every time the modes, standards, and points of view with regard to life change, the curriculum slowly but surely shows corresponding variations. The pressures and sanctions of life seek expression in the things that are taught in the schools. This does not mean that they are always right or always best, for many of them are local, temporary, and ephemeral in character, and should be resisted. On the other hand, some of them are so universal and represent such deep-seated aspirations and needs that refusal to respond to them would be tantamount to intellectual suicide.

Of this we may be reasonably certain: history, valuable as it is, is not a safe guide for determining progress except as it may reveal trends or tendencies. The force of precedent, which has been and still is the cloak of many — especially of the lawyer — weakens in the face of new methods, new techniques, and a new spirit. This is particularly true in these stirring days when life is taking on forms strikingly unlike anything the world has ever seen. Apparently no one can have an adequate conception of the significance and place of the modern university in this new world without first knowing something about that world itself.

To a university man, nothing exceeds in significance the growth in knowledge that has occurred in recent years. When Bacon said, "I have taken all knowledge to be my province," he was living in a world that had not yet felt the stimulating effects of scientific achievement. The universe of Francis Bacon was narrow and fixed. Today the astronomers have revealed to us new stellar infinities and declared that the heavens are composed of universe upon universe; likewise the geologists have penetrated the earth's surface and the archaeologists and anthropologists have written much of the story of its prehistoric life. The hieroglyphics of the ancients have been deciphered. History has been carried back thousands if not tens of thousands of years. The biologists, embryologists, anatomists, and botanists are revealing processes of life of the most astonishing character. Physicists such as Maxwell, Hertz, Thomson, Roentgen, Curie, Michelson, Einstein, and Millikan have ventured into the unknown and discovered truth that is revolutionizing the thought and life of men. Psychologists, sociologists, philosophers, and a myriad of others belonging to the regimental army of scientists and scholars have contributed so greatly to the sum total of human knowledge that today no man can say with Bacon, "I have taken all knowledge to be my province."

Never did men engaged in educational work walk so humbly, experience such self-abnegation of spirit, or possess such frail wisdom as they do now when they seek to assess and transmit the enormous accumulation of knowledge mankind has gathered since the days of Bacon.

97

The most casual searcher after knowledge feels profoundly the changes this new knowledge has wrought in the life of the people, while the diligent and faithful searcher stands almost in awe of it. The ability to think is what it has always been, but scholarship, in the sense of mastery over a few and a working knowledge of many fields, requires infinitely greater effort and concentration today than ever before, and few there are who attain it.

The expansion of knowledge, like all other human progress, is due to the insistent urge for achievement that inheres in the human breast. Man is dissatisfied and wants something better. Civilization is but a continuing process of overlaying the more primitive and elemental practices of yesterday with the improvements which human genius is making today and will make tomorrow. The desire for improvement keeps life in motion from day to day and from hour to hour, and the improvements themselves, as they come into general use, modify the intellectual and emotional life of people everywhere. Humanity, at any given moment, seems like a glacier, slow-moving; but when the movements are compared the former is like a swift-moving stream, quickened into action by waters from new sources.

But my interest just now is confined largely to showing that changes in the world of knowledge have placed man in possession of a whole series of new

freedoms and have imposed upon him heavier responsibilities if not new ones. The miracle of new power
which man now possesses by having penetrated beyond the border lines into hitherto unknown regions,
by having dispelled ignorance with learning, displaced
superstition with knowledge and rule of thumb with
scientific scrutiny and method, has liberated man's
mind and emancipated him from much of the ancient
drudgery.

This emancipation from drudgery has expressed itself in a number of practical ways, perhaps the most
significant of which is the control he has gained over
his material environment. Instead of being the crea-
ture of grinding toil, he now has countless machines
to do his work for him. President Scott of North-
western University has shown that the maximum of
surplus power possessed by freemen at the peak of
prosperity in Babylon, Egypt, Greece, and Rome was
the equivalent of two slaves, while today, as a result
of the inventiveness of man, there is in America the
equivalent of 175 mechanical slaves for every person.
President Scott further says, "The American who today possesses the equivalent of 175-slave power will
probably possess double that amount in a few years.
He is constantly improving the methods, the conditions, and the implements for availing himself of that
power. According to our census report of 1869, over
50 per cent of our power was animal and less than 50

per cent of it mechanical, but at the present time it is approximately 2.5 per cent animal and 97.5 per cent mechanical power."

Men differ enormously in their views with regard to what this means to mankind. Certain it is that while machines greatly increase man's productive power on the one hand, they multiply his wants on the other. The luxuries and superluxuries of yesterday are but ordinary commodities of today. And many new occupations and trades have been created with the advent of the machine. For example, the World Almanac estimates that the automobile man power of the United States now calls for 3,732,000 men and women, all added in a few years' time to the American labor budget. As Stuart Chase has said, it takes a staggering amount of work to live up to the demands of our vendors; and it takes a staggering budget to fabricate their goods.

It seems that everything, when once made, must be sold and used — radios must be listened to, movies seen, chewing gum chewed, cigarettes smoked, and cosmetics spread on lips and cheeks. The more we produce, the more the advertiser insists that we need. Even Henry Ford has declared that men should not attempt to save anything until they are forty or forty-five years of age — that everything they earn at earlier ages over and above the simplest necessities of living should be turned back into industry and commerce for the purpose of increasing trade. It would appear that not thrift but greater spending, not saving but more selling, are ideals of the modern world.

The coming of the machine into modern life has not only modified old forms of labor; it has in turn created a new world. I have seen this transformation take place within my own lifetime. My boyhood was spent on a farm and in a small town. I can remember seeing my own grandmother dip tallow candles; I saw her card the wool, spin the yarn, knit the socks. My own mother quilted quilts, made clothing for the family, did the baking; while on the farm the reaping was done with the sickle, the cradle, and the dropper. We cut our own wood, split our own rails, cleaned our grain, and in a thousand ways found employment from sun-up until dark. Everyone learned to do many things and no one thought of refusing to try any of them. The town where I spent some of my boyhood was small but a place where everyone could exercise his initiative to the utmost. All one needed to do in order to be in business in the morning was to hang out his shingle the evening before. There were no telephones, no good roads, no automobiles, no chain stores; in fact, the country peddler drove by our farm every week and exchanged coffee, sugar, and gingham for our eggs and butter and my game.

Now, in that same community, modern machinery is found on the farms, men work fewer hours a day, macadam roads lead in every direction, automobiles and telephones are found in every home and radios in most of them; chain stores and a chain creamery occupy permanent sites in the town, and soon the banks will be a part of a chain banking system. There is more activity, more moving of materials, more speeding up of effort, more organization of forces and processes, more building and rebuilding. The community thinks it is progressive and it is. It is typical of tens of thousands of other communities throughout America. It enjoys having men of my generation talk about the looms and the smithies but it regards them as relics of an ancient and unprogressive past.

Josiah Royce in his *World and the Individual* says that every gain is always accompanied by its corresponding loss. That I believe to be true in this instance. Certainly the spirit of craftsmanship has been disappearing with the advent of the new order and with the coming of the machine. Even in those ancient countries where the handicrafts have thrived and prospered, they are now rapidly disappearing before the invasion of twentieth-century civilization. And strange things are happening in America: oriental rugs are now manufactured in Philadelphia; Sicilian, Grecian, and Turkestan art is being duplicated in quantity in various cities; antique furniture will be made while you wait; the linens, laces, luncheon cloths, and the like which the Russian peasant and the Belgian household have produced with such artistic accuracy and beauty by hand are now made by the thousands in factories. Hand production is so slow that we are unwilling to wait for it. We want everything and we want it now. As a result everything is produced in quantities — furniture, clothing, food, heat, light, and transportation facilities.

Mass production, even though it tends to crystallize things into a single design and may at times put a brake on technical progress as well as craftsmanship, is nevertheless a dominant characteristic of the times. The benefits mankind derives from it are so numerous and so vast that few would think of giving them up to return to the simpler life of earlier days. The hours of necessary labor have been reduced and the returns man gets from his labor are pleasing to him. Poverty has been reduced and the standards of living have been elevated. Life has been enriched and made easier and more comfortable.

With the transformation of industry and the expansion of production there has come another phenomenon, namely, organization on a grand scale. The collective man is partly the product of specialization of function, and specialization of function has arisen because knowledge has become so great and skills so numerous and technical that no one man can hope to master many of them. Furthermore, those who are the beneficiaries of this knowledge and of these skills demand the highest possible grade of expert service, and this can be had only through these organizations.

The movement is revealed everywhere and in everything. Even the professions have not escaped. Doctors, for example, have been forced to organize for diagnosis and treatment. It is an inescapable part of the new order. The tendency toward organized medicine has come just as big business, chain stores, and financial aggregations have come. Some of the changes brought to society by this movement in the last few decades are hospitals, paid clinics, diagnostic clinics, treatment clinics, public health work, and group practice. All these have changed the status of the doctor.

One begins to wonder what the future has in store for the family physician or the general practitioner. How shall we keep this valuable man, with his personality, his human contacts, his cheering smile, his encouraging words at the sickbed, his deep understanding of human nature and his air of hope? No one knows the answer and yet everyone admits that it would be a great loss to the human race if he were to vanish. He may have to go; it seems likely that he will.

The same thing that is happening in medicine is happening in other professions. What has become of the independent editor, with the graceful or vitriolic pen, who dared to express himself on public issues with only the public in mind? He is being absorbed by the chain paper. What has become of the outstanding lawyer in this new scheme of life? He has become a part of a team. What has become of the individual teacher who used to pass out wisdom in the little red schoolhouse? He has become a part of a great educational association which now gathers youth into magnificent consolidated schools. What has become of the individual professor who insisted on individual merit as the sole basis of recognition? He has become a member of a protective association. Even the rural merchant is disappearing, and the farmers he serves are being drawn into a social organization.

Specialization and consolidation have hit the church. The smaller churches are being absorbed by the larger, and the work of the minister is being differentiated into many lines with a specialist in charge of each. That old-fashioned parson who lived among his people and broke daily bread with them is in danger of disappearing, along with his friend and co-worker, the family doctor.

Thus it is that the relations of men in every walk of life are being altered. Apparently we shall soon be a salaried nation, depending largely on organization rather than individual resourcefulness for our livelihood.

The movement for scientific management, orderly organization, and the elimination of waste is not confined to industry, big business, and the professions. It has invaded statecraft, both at home and abroad. The one thing common throughout the nations is the development of life from individualism to a closely knit social organization. In Italy, for example, the Fascist is not considered an entity but merely a fraction of a greater whole. Here, perhaps, the philosophy of social organization in the political field is carried to its highest development, although it resembles in a number of fundamental respects the control of Russia by the Communists. A member of the Communist party must accept and follow the judgment of the majority no matter what his own views may be. Furthermore, the communistic doctrine is based on the assumptions that there shall be no privileged class and that all property belongs to the state.

These sweeping transformations clearly reveal that the center of gravity of human interest has been shifting from politics to economics and from individual enterprise to vast organization. Everywhere men are becoming increasingly more concerned with production, distribution, and consumption of wealth and the development of new kinds of power. President Butler recently declared that there is today in the world no great poet, no great philosopher, and no great religious leader. Be this as it may, the intellectual forces which have shaped history in the past have had to do with the "worth of the individual, with his knowledge, his faith; with his self-expression for achievement, for liberty to live his own life, to shape his own thought, to express his own opinions, and to be the center of his own personal world." At such times interest in political institutions and great organizations lagged, while interest in poetry, art, philosophy, religion flourished. With the coming of the steam engine and the utilization of electricity, the tide of human interests began to shift from country to city, from the handicrafts to the machines, from individual effort to organized effort, from the humanities to science.

Mr. Beard and others in *Whither Mankind*, commenting upon this very matter, declare that the omnipotence of the collective man as contrasted with the feebleness of the individual man stands out in bold relief as the most striking characteristic of modern times.

Within certain limits in this paragraph I speak in terms of emphasis rather than in terms of inclusiveness. It is true that the youth of today do not establish themselves in business as their fathers did; they get positions or jobs. Today their success depends largely on speed, rather than on skill or knowledge. Initiative instead of being rewarded is likely to be interpreted as a sign of inefficiency. The danger is that these young persons will fall victims to routine types of work and develop clerical minds. Efficiency is the modern pagan god before whom they bow in order that dividends may be paid. Those who guide the activities of the struggling young apprentice are frequently a thousand miles away. They know him by his reports rather than as a personality. If he invests in property, he invests in stock, but a few shares of stock certificates filed away in a lock box are a poor substitute for an enterprise in which he may have a personal interest, and of which the success depends upon his resourcefulness and initiative.

Count Keyserling in his *Travel Diary of a Philosopher* presents a gloomy view. He says, "In America the individual is simply ceasing to exist; all development is moving in the direction of standardization; intellectual interests as such play hardly a part in the life at large; all values are weighed by their practical application and by their application to the collective benefit."

Walter Pitkin in *The Twilight of the American Mind* maintains that by 1975 America will no longer provide opportunities sufficient to engage or employ the "Best Minds"; life will have become too mechanized or stereotyped.

Thus it is that we begin to realize that in this new world there is in process a conflict between freedom, initiative, and independence on the one hand and direction, submission, and control on the other. It is the conflict between the individual and the social order, between the worker and his work, between the subject and the nation. It presents a philosophic dilemma as old as the human race but raised now to a magnitude and power never before witnessed.

The late Dr. E. E. Slosson, the director of Science Service, gave this warning: "The last few years have made it manifest that in our civilization the mechanical forces have got ahead of the moral (and intellectual) forces. . . . The physical sciences have evidently been developed so far beyond the political (and social) forces as to constitute a menace to civilization. The modern man, like the Arabian fisherman, has liberated from the bottle genii that he does not know how to control."

Stuart Chase, however, comes to the rescue with the challenge: "This is the last great adventure — the boldest, most exhilarating, most dangerous adventure that ever challenged the intelligence and spirit of mankind. From our brains have sprung a billion horses, now running wild and almost certain sooner or later to run amuck. Where are the riders with the whirling rope; where are the light-hearted youth to mount, be thrown, and rise to mount again?"

And may it not be that we, blinded by the philosophy of submission, have overlooked or have failed to appraise at their proper worth the new types of freedom, economic and intellectual, we have acquired? Men today, if they think at all, must think in larger units than ever before. The horizon has been pushed back, the sky overhead has been broadened. The human voice can be heard around the earth by millions, and those who are miles away can be seen while they speak. Truly the world is growing smaller and its people closer together.

An increasing amount of consideration is being given to the compensations of science and the results which a machine world entails in education, art, religion. President Hoover in his acceptance speech, while glorifying the conveniences and power of applied science, pointed out a few pertinent truths: "Economic advancement is not an end in itself. . . . A people or government to which these [spiritual] values are not real because they are not tangible, is in peril. . . . Our purpose is to build in this nation a human society, not an economic system."

What is to happen in America is purely a question of psychology. Already there have been great advances in efficiency, in government, in social justice, in social welfare, security, knowledge, aesthetic appreciation. This is but "the dawn, not the dusk, of the gods." And the gods will never sense danger so long as man aspires to divinity by the spiritual route, but they will begin to raise their Olympic eyebrows when material prosperity is counted on to blaze a new path to heaven.

Whether this industrial era in which we are living and apparently the one which lies just ahead of us shall be primarily economic depends upon the state of mind that accompanies them. If the gain-seeking motive dominates, then it is primarily economic; if the public service dominates, then it is not. "A part of the punishment of a man who is dominated by the gain-seeking motive resides in the fact that he never knows what he has lost." The gain-seeking motive is always self-destroying, while the public service motive is always self-building. One cripples the imagination, narrows the vision, and disintegrates the soul, while the other stirs the imagination, enlarges the vision, and makes the soul still more worthy. Clearly the test of an industrial age is the uses man makes of his emancipation from ancient drudgery and from the heavy burdens he once bore.

Much time has elapsed since I referred to universities and their work and I fear you will feel that I have strayed permanently from the task I set for this occasion. But such is not the case. It is a fact, I believe, that every new economic freedom has released human energy and new spiritual forces, and as a result the people have turned to the schools, colleges, and universities for guidance. True, they have not always found what they wished, for there are institutions that represent a social order long since decadent. Benefactions totaling hundreds of millions and revenues running into still larger figures are provided annually for the support of the universities. This in itself is evidence of appreciation and confidence in these institutions. To do their work well they must live in an atmosphere of freedom, undominated and uncontrolled by any particular group or interest. They must be free to seek the truth and to teach it, free to study and interpret the forces of life and to expound them; otherwise they cannot be lighthouses or dynamos for those who seek light or desire power. And they must be open to the thousands who clamor at their doors seeking that background of knowledge so essential to understanding life. The rancor of the market place and cries of the forum must never disturb their tranquillity of mind if they are to think on life and to interpret its meanings.

Man's capacity for culture has been raised by the new standards of living and the amazing development of communication, travel, and industry. He has more leisure. The best music, drama, and literature are now within the reach of everyone. In the field of art, beauty in new forms is constantly being created and displayed on every hand. Never before was there such need for instruction in the humanities as an antidote to industrialism and never before were so many responding to the call.

Both the flexibility and the comprehensiveness of knowledge have been increased, and science has revealed that in the indistinct areas lying between the various fields of knowledge are unsolved problems of such portentous significance as to stagger the imagination.

If men wish to do so they can become members of an industrial slavery quite as abject as that of ancient days. Or they can extend the period of human infancy and provide more education for those who are to serve tomorrow; and they can recognize that education is no longer something to be confined to youth and that the movement for adult education is of as great social and ethical significance as the movement for the education of youth. If leisure is used solely or largely for the gratification of pleasure and personal satisfaction, then the cause of civilization will not be advanced by it. The great inheritances of the race are not found in capital, in vast organizations, or in mass production, but in those spiritual possessions which should guide us in ways of tolerance and of co-operation at all times. In such ways the world should be changed for man's benefit. Economy, efficiency, and organization must be substituted for waste, inefficiency, and chaos; plenty, health, and education for famine, disease, and ignorance.

The schoolmen of this generation and those who are interested in the ideals they represent cannot sit on the side lines and watch this onward sweep of things without civilization paying a heavy toll for their neglect. Whether our children shall be subjects or freemen in thought, whether personality shall be stifled by technique, whether knowledge shall be synthesized, made more flexible and of broader application, whether leisure shall lift man off the plane of the sensuous to higher moral and spiritual conceptions of life — these are matters of supreme importance. Not less industry but more, not less organization but more, not less science but more, is what we need if industry and organization and science are dedicated to making man master of himself and not the slave of the machine. In the final analysis, the only poverty that is odious to face is the poverty of life itself.

VII

TWO WAYS OF IMPROVING THE STATE UNIVERSITIES

Presidential address delivered before the National Association of State Universities, Washington, D. C., November 19, 1930

THE civilization of America is built from the natural resources of America. When the pioneers came they found what seemed to be limitless natural resources. There were great forests extending far into the distance; there were broad acres awaiting only the touch of the plow and the hand of man to yield rich harvests; there were enormous deposits of ore awaiting only the coming of the scientist to produce the machinery of civilization; there were rivers whose water power was unharnessed.

We pay tribute to the pioneer who moved from east to west across this continent, facing all of the dangers of a new country filled with unfriendly inhabitants and infested with wild life. The life of the pioneer is a life of romance. It appeals to old and young alike. But there followed in his wake those who made his home sites more secure, who built railroads, constructed bridges, erected schoolhouses and churches, who laid the basis for a new civilization. Frontier after frontier was conquered. The "boundless" forests of New England, of Virginia, of Michigan, of Minnesota disappeared in turn. Today most of our building material is shipped from far away Oregon, or Washington, or Canada. As one travels through New England and Virginia today, he is struck by the great number of abandoned farms. Census reports just issued show that the number of farms in practically every state is steadily declining. The rich top soil which man found, and which he exploited without giving a proper return, has been destroyed. The same kind of waste has been practiced in the coal, copper, and iron mines. With the cutting of the forests there has been a decrease of rainfall and a drying up of the swamps, a lowering of the streams, and a consequent disappearance of much of the game and wild life of the country.

But it is true, nevertheless, that these forests and mines, this rich top soil, and the other resources of nature have furnished us with the wealth which enabled us to establish our present level of civilization. They have supplied the resources which have made possible our great urban centers, our unparalleled means of communication, our great electrical development, and a thousand and one other things that contribute to the comfort and pleasure of our people. The wealth derived directly and indirectly from the riches of nature has paid the bills for all our social and welfare work. It has helped to establish and maintain charitable and penal institutions, and it has been largely responsible for the great progress which America has made in the development of her educational system.

America derived the funds to establish and maintain her standard of living, her forms of institutional life, including education, from agriculture and its products, from the forests and their products, from the mines and their products, from the development of the streams and their products.

Now America faces a new situation. There are no more forests to speak of. It will take fifty years or more of care and cultivation to produce a pine forest of commercial value in Minnesota. The mines are being exhausted. The top soil is becoming thinner and every year more fertilizer is required to make it productive. The number of farms is decreasing. Water power, to be sure, is being developed, but there is less water to be harnessed than there was a hundred years ago. Meantime civilization has become more complex, its problems more numerous and more difficult of solution. The important question which the American people face is, How shall the civilization which we have established now be maintained and advanced? Certainly we cannot use the methods of our forefathers if there is nothing to which we can apply them; we cannot cut timber if there is no timber to cut; we shall not be interested in mining if there is no ore to be mined.

Perhaps it may be said that we are no longer dependent directly upon nature for our material development, and in a certain sense that is true, for man has, through inventions, devised thousands of new ways of producing wealth and of contributing to his comfort — ways that sometimes seem remotely related to the processes of nature. Man, for example, has organized capital and built machines which have greatly increased his power of production. Yet the fact remains that these have been achieved in large part because of the supplies nature so lavishly furnished him. In achieving these things it is obvious, even to the most casual observer, that man has been wasteful of nature's supplies; now he must turn to means to aid him if he is to maintain and to advance civilization.

When Mr. Julius Rosenwald created a great foundation in Chicago recently, he issued a statement to the effect that he expected the entire sum to be spent within the next twenty-five years. He said he believed that each generation should spend its own riches largely in improving conditions for itself. This I believe to be essentially an unsound doctrine. To a very large extent we have built this civilization from capital which we found. In destroying that capital and in utilizing its products for our own personal benefit, we lay upon the generations that follow a heavier burden to maintain and advance civilization. There is current in America a doctrine that because each generation has got along fairly well, the next one can do the same. We say we have provided for ourselves; why, therefore, should we make any provision for the next generation? We assume that it will be as easy for it to make progress as it has been for us. That, too, in my opinion, is a thoroughly blind and selfish position to take with regard to the welfare of the social order. If we establish a basis for civilization and assume that those who follow after us will find other sources of wealth to maintain it, time may prove that we have reckoned without the costs.

It is my opinion that the course of civilization in the future, certainly so far as its material benefits are concerned, will depend upon what happens in the laboratories of men. New wealth may not be so easy to obtain in the future as it has been in the past. It seems clear that the next generation may find that it must supply its wants by relying upon research rather than upon bounteous nature. It will be more expensive to maintain and advance civilization through science than it has been to advance and maintain it on the profits of nature.

Our generation and those that preceded it have drawn heavily upon their capital assets for current operations and expenses. By capital assets I mean the measured resources which nature gave mankind. They have converted these into money and spent it. But very little of this capital has been set aside as an endowment. Almost no provision has been made for future growth. We have gone on cutting our trees, exhausting our mines, and devastating our soil with little thought or consideration for the welfare of the next generation.

One cannot say that no consideration has been given to it, for both the federal and state governments have set aside some lands and timber for the endowment of education, and in more recent years the legislatures of a number of states have provided that a certain share of the occupational and royalty taxes shall be converted into endowment funds for education. But the endowment funds are too small to be especially significant.

If the leaders of the various states are interested in building a civilization where there will be little or no poverty, where men will enjoy all the known comforts of life, where they will have the benefit of the most modern developments in medicine, surgery, and nursing, where literature may flourish, where education will be universal, where science will be stimulated and creative work will be encouraged to the very limit, they will not be satisfied with the biennial appropriations their legislatures grant. They will take steps looking toward the establishment of great endowments, the income from which shall be used for these purposes.

One state, Texas, has already taken steps toward the achievement of this end. She has made provision for the building of an endowment for her university, so I am informed, which will amount to two hundred million dollars. This means that there will be a great people in Texas whose welfare and interests will be studied and served, whose problems will be examined and solved by great scholars and scientists on the staff at the University of Texas.

Not long ago I heard a distinguished gentleman say that the state universities of this country could not compete with the great private universities; that the private institutions, with their endowments and the increasing millions which come to them annually in the form of gifts from their friends and alumni, will make it impossible for the state universities ever to compete with them. This is a confession that the states are willing that their universities shall be commonplace, that they shall not exercise the leadership to which they have aspired; for, if they cannot compete successfully with the private universities, they will never be able to attract or retain persons of distinction on their own staffs. There are very few states, if any, that are not wealthier than all the alumni of any of the private universities. There are undoubtedly some states that have more wealth than all the alumni of all the private universities combined. Furthermore, there is no reason why the states should not do for their universities what the alumni are doing for private institutions, that is, set out deliberately to aid them by building large endowments year by year. This can be done without impairing in any way the control of the people of the state, through their legislature, over the universities; and furthermore, it will lay the basis for continuing and advancing civilization generation after generation.

In addition to the alumni of private institutions, the great foundations of this country appear to be more interested in financing and endowing private institutions than in financing and endowing state universities. A study of the contributions to higher education made during the last seven years by the General Education Board, the Carnegie Corporation, the Rockefeller Foundation, the Commonwealth Fund, and the Laura Spelman Rockefeller Memorial reveals the very interesting fact that 91.5 per cent of their contributions during this period have been made to private universities and to private colleges, 8 per cent to state universities, 0.1 per cent to municipal universities, and 0.4 per cent to state colleges. It also reveals the fact that these grants are made to a small number of institutions. These have been described recently as "prestige" institutions. It would appear from the distribution of funds by the foundations during this period that there is some basis for the opinion that they are not genuinely interested in research or higher education as such, but that they are interested in research and higher education in a limited number of these prestige institutions.

The baneful effects of this policy upon higher education in general — if it be a policy and if it be continued — are perfectly obvious. Consideration must be given to this important matter by the various states and by individual philanthropists if public welfare is to be conserved and advanced.

There is no good reason why the great foundations should not finance and endow projects at state institutions if conditions highly favorable for carrying on these projects prevail at these institutions. In fact, the stimulation of intellectual effort and provision for permanent centers for research at various places across the country, in both public and private institutions, are highly desirable in the interests of higher education and the public welfare. But this is not the policy of these foundations; at any rate it does not appear to be their policy. The foundations should join with the states just as they do with the alumni and others interested in the private universities in providing endowments at state institutions for the purpose of insuring social progress.

Every state that looks to the future will take steps to provide for its progressive development. In doing so it must be willing to spend millions for research and conservation; it must provide endowments of tens of millions rather than hundreds of thousands.

In the second chapter of this paper I wish to speak of another matter which I think will contribute to the distinction of the state universities. Endowments I believe to be necessary, but it will take time to build them. Meantime there is no good reason why the state universities should not give careful consideration to the allocation of functions. There is, as we know, a marked tendency in America for higher institutions of learning to duplicate each other. Hitherto institutional respectability has seemed to require this. And yet in this very tendency there is a weakness, if not a menace, to American education. It could easily be shown that the refusal on the part of higher institutions of learning to consider the allocation of functions results in inefficiency and mediocrity. Not all colleges and universities can be distinguished in everything or in many things.

Some of the duplication of work and effort in the universities is both socially necessary and desirable; that, for example, which provides training in the common essentials of an educated citizenry. But that which is dedicated to special fields of learning and to limited sections of knowledge would prosper more if it were, by agreement, concentrated in fewer places. Research in limited fields and sections of learning and knowledge could be carried on in a few places, the several institutions cooperating rather than competing as at present.

A few illustrations will make clear the lack of national and state policy with regard to this problem. The federal government has made grants from time to time for the promotion of higher education. These grants have often been made and certainly they have been distributed on artificial bases that had little or no relation to need. Money for agricultural and engineering experiment stations has been distributed to each state in equal sums. The same practice, in general, has been followed with regard to the distribution of funds for the promotion of other types of research or education in which the federal government is interested. In other words, this money is distributed to states without regard to whether or not they possess the conditions necessary for its wise expenditure. A typical illustration will suffice.

Washington and Idaho receive practically the same amount of money from the federal government. The land grant college in Washington is located eight miles from the University of Idaho. Both institutions have all the departments that a college of agriculture is supposed to have. Each maintains a school of forestry and each maintains a school of mines. They are trying to serve the same agricultural, forest, and mining area. If it were possible, under federal legislation, for Idaho to limit her functions to certain fields and Washington to limit hers to others, abler men could be obtained at each of these institutions and the whole area which the two universities are supposed to serve would profit thereby.

How many schools of forestry or how many schools of mining or how many genuine agricultural experiment stations the United States actually needs, the country has never really dared to say. The states have gone on accepting the money which the federal government has handed them for forestry, or mining, or agriculture, even though they may not have possessed facilities competent to carry on high-grade research. In other words, the money has not been distributed to the men who have already demonstrated their fitness and ability to do or to direct the research work which our national welfare requires. As a matter of fact, many of these men may not be in state institutions at all; they may be in private universities. It has been the general practice and policy of the federal government to distribute its money to public rather than to private institutions. The consideration, however, on the part of the national government of the allocation of functions and the distribution of money according to areas and according to the location of men competent to carry on research would result in a wiser expenditure of funds. Fewer centers, properly located, thoroughly equipped, and unusually well staffed, will produce more in the long run than a large number of centers inadequately equipped and poorly staffed.

It may be said that federal money has been distributed partly for the purpose of stimulating research in certain areas, but research cannot be stimulated in this way. It is possible to build a building and equip it and call it an institute of research of some sort, but it takes more than buildings and equipment to produce research. Now and then there may be an isolated case of a man of rare ability located at one of these more remote experiment stations. Superior men would be found in greater numbers, however, if the experiment stations were consolidated and if the problems upon which they are at work were related to the interests of geographical areas. In other words, the federal government, if it desires to have its money used to promote the common welfare in a most effective manner, should disregard state and political lines and arrange for its distribution on the basis of the common problems found in given areas and regions.

Not only has the federal government failed to exercise foresight and wisdom in the distribution of money for educational purposes, but the states themselves have been perhaps equally derelict in this matter. The distribution of federal moneys has been controlled largely by politics rather than by educational needs. The appropriation of state moneys has been controlled to a very large extent by local pride and prestige.

There has been a struggle on the part of the state universities to acquire academic respectability. This, for the greater part, has consisted in the number and variety rather than in the quality of offerings.

It would be the part of wisdom, so it seems to me, for those institutions located in a given region to join in outlining their programs, defining their functions, and allocating their responsibilities. To be specific, the state universities of Illinois, Iowa, Ohio, Michigan, Wisconsin, and Minnesota might agree that Minnesota should become the great library center for the Scandinavian cultures and that all these other institutions should assist the University of Minnesota in becoming such a center. They might agree that the University of Michigan should become a great center for the Romance languages and that all the other institutions should assist Michigan in becoming such a center. If this plan were followed and extended, each of these universities might become the leading library center for some one of the great fields of learning. Each of these universities would, of course, have in its library all those books and pamphlets and other materials which are necessary for undergraduate instruction and for the common culture of people everywhere.

Again, it would seem that cooperation is possible in carrying on experiments of direct interest to agriculture. There is already considerable cooperation in this field. It is doubtful, however, whether the large-scale stock feeding experiments are necessary at Wisconsin, Minnesota, Ames (Iowa), and Illinois; at any rate, it scarcely seems that they need to be carried on simultaneously. Experiments of this sort require large sums of money. It should be possible for those who are interested in the stock feeding experiments at these various institutions to be constituted a cooperating committee with the understanding that the members of this committee would direct the experiments and check all the results. What has been said with regard to stock feeding applies with equal force to poultry raising, to the various aspects of animal husbandry, to the study of plants and insects injurious to crops, to the diseases of animals, and the like.

If this plan were extended, it is conceivable that institutions would send students who have received certain fundamental training to another university for more advanced training. It is conceivable that the states would provide scholarships which would enable them to send men from Minnesota to Wisconsin or Illinois or Iowa for certain training, while Wisconsin, Illinois, and Iowa in turn would send men to Minnesota for other types of training. Such a plan would insure a better and higher grade of scholastic work; it would promote and encourage research; it would insure greater permanency on the part of the staff; and it would enable the institutions to pay the abler men more than they now receive, for with a limitation of functions some money would be released which could be used to improve the quality of the staff.

Some of the private universities have already appointed committees to consider this very matter. I know of one group of institutions that has appointed a committee of research in the various medical fields with a view to emphasizing to a greater extent than hitherto the researches to be carried on at each. For example, one of them may become the cancer center, another the eye, ear, nose, and throat center, and so on. This means that the private institutions associated in this manner will not appeal to the same sources for funds for the same purpose.

When the colleges and universities of America free themselves from that fetish of respectability which requires them to offer instruction that their neighbors are offering; when they cease to compete for the purpose of salving their consciences; when they decline to appeal for money because someone else has something; when they discard that selfish tradition to which they cling and before which they worship — the tradition that those colleges are best which present the greatest variety of offerings — then college and university instruction in America will be conducted on a higher plane than ever before. Whenever the public is able to rise above state lines, whenever its legislators refuse to think of the political consequences of their acts, then the universities will receive that encouragement, sanction, and support that they should have in carrying out the kind of program here outlined.

It is my opinion that the next ten years or less will see many steps taken in both these directions, that is, the establishment and growth of state endowments for state universities and the allocation of functions among the institutions themselves.

VIII

EDUCATIONAL TRENDS IN THE
UNIVERSITY OF MINNESOTA

An address delivered on the twenty-fifth anniversary
of the founding of the College of Education of the
University of Minnesota, April 16, 1930

A UNIVERSITY is a human institution. It originates in the stimulating soil of human needs and exists to satisfy human wants. It redefines its aims, modifies its programs, and sets new problems for itself as the social order in which and for which it lives changes its nature and its being. Continually subjected to new pressures and new demands, no university ever remains the same year after year. On the other hand no university can or should respond to every request for service; there must be a continuity and a stability to its aims and work. It is not always easy to secure and to maintain this stability and especially has that been true in recent years.

During the last decade American institutions of higher learning have felt with increasing force the demands of special groups that have desired to use them for their own ends. Many of these groups are actuated by motives that their followers believe to be entirely worthy. They are anxious to save the universities from their sins or from what they, without any real knowledge of university life or traditions, assume are sins, or they desire to have some special service performed that will help them to revive a dying business or to increase the dividends of a successful enterprise. Sometimes the leaders of these groups are enthusiasts in the field of religion who wish to prevent the teaching of evolution. Sometimes they are conscientious conservatives who insist that biological science shall suppress the conclusions or implications which the patient search for truth has made logically inevitable. Other groups, under the appealing name of patriotism, demand a teaching of history which may pander to our national vanity but which is entirely inconsistent with the facts. In the interest of economy, some have devised political machinery placing the financial control of their universities with boards or officials in no way related to the actual administration of the universities, thus disregarding the well established principle that the educational functions of a university cannot be dissociated from its financial control. Others have deliberately, openly, and avowedly sought the control of universities for political purposes; and still others have dignified, exalted, and offered such abundant support to extracurricular activities that the real educational functions of the university have suffered.

A university, as we have said, must change to conform with the spirit of the times. The leaders of these groups recognize this principle; they think, in most instances certainly, that they are dominated by altruistic rather than by selfish motives; they maintain that they represent public rather than minority opinion. It must be clear that there will never come a time, indeed there should never come a time, when universities will not be subject to such pressures. No university can ever isolate itself entirely from the world in which it lives. Every expansion of its scope and enlargement of its functions has come in response to some need and to some new sanction.

On the other hand it must be equally clear that, even though a university is a social institution, it is engaged in a constant struggle for the right to exist as a university, and that it cannot exist as a university in any genuine sense if it is borne hither and yon by the winds of minority opinion. A true university will be steadfast in its purposes and ideals; it will seek to secure the common good, not the welfare of a few. It will be characterized by tolerance of opinion, by freedom of speech and action, by unrestricted search for truth, and by the right to teach that truth once it has been found. Every problem pertaining to human welfare will furnish it with food for thought and research. Every activity, even the so-called extra-curricular activities, will fit into and play its part in developing the educational program of the institution.

When men sell a mercantile establishment, a manufacturing plant, a newspaper, or a bank, they charge something for its good will. What constitutes the good will of a university? Is it to be found in the opinion of transient groups that wish to have some special service performed? Is it to be found in a minority group of a few hundred that presumes to represent the opinion of thousands? Is it to be found among those who would sacrifice educational standards for a good football team? The good will of a university is not found among any of these. The good will of a university is that public opinion which insists that the university shall ceaselessly dedicate its efforts to greater scholastic achievement and to the discovery of new knowledge. This kind of good will recognizes that whatever attention the university gives to matters of human character and to recreational affairs is for the purpose of insuring better intellectual results.

The good will of a university is not something that can be bought and sold; all the people are shareholders in it and all participate in its dividends. The dividends consist of a thousand things that make life more worth living. The search for these things and the dissemination of information about them require that the universities shall protect the lamps of learning from the biased and prejudiced opinions of those who would divert their university from those things which lead to intellectual righteousness and to public good. Any good will, no matter how much it may flatter your university, no matter how obsequiously it may seek its services, no matter how loudly it may proclaim its loyalty, if it ignores this point of view, is not the true good will that we desire.

What I have been trying to say is that the most important trend in university circles today is the struggle for the right to exist as universities. The fires of criticism have been burning more brightly and with greater intensity in the last decade than at any other time in American history. The right to exist and the freedom to enjoy that right were never more essential to the life of a university than today. Those who believe in these ideals must ever be on their guard if their universities are not to become playhouses, social clubs, or the agents of special interests. This right to live on the higher intellectual levels is more important than money, more important than numbers of students, more important than the personnel of the university's administration, more important than all other considerations combined.

The right to exist as a university carries with it the obligation to live; that is, to maintain the standards and ideals of a university. And in this regard I may be pardoned, I hope, if I say that the University of Minnesota is taking some forward, if not unique, steps. One of these is the selection of students competent to do university work. The University of Minnesota is a state university; it is doubtful if it has the right to exclude graduates of approved high schools. And yet it is a well recognized fact that students occasionally are graduated from high school who are not capable of doing satisfactory college work. How these students get through high school will probably always remain one of the unsolved human mysteries. I have thought, sometimes, that writers of modern detective stories might apply their genius to this problem with profit to humanity. It is barely possible that the graduation of an occasional moron from high school is due to the desire on the part of the high school teachers to cultivate the spirit of Christianity among college teachers; having suffered so many years themselves, they seek that companionship in humility by making it necessary for college teachers to suffer with them.

The superintendents, principals, and high school teachers of the state, working in cooperation with the University of Minnesota and later with the Association of Minnesota Colleges, began testing high school seniors several years ago with a view to discovering those who possess college ability. This movement is unique among the states of the Union. Last year, tests were given in more than twenty centers to more than 10,000 high school seniors.

This testing has been carried on long enough so that we are now able to state with considerable exactness what its results are. While the tests have never been used as a basis for denying students entrance to the university, they have, nevertheless, operated as a selective agency. This is shown by the fact that the quality of the students entering the university has improved from year to year since the tests were introduced. The success of the testing movement is to be attributed largely to the fact that the results of the tests are turned over to superintendents and high school principals to be used by them in advising students as to whether they should go to college. It is not claimed that the advice which can thus be given is one hundred per cent accurate, nor are those whose ratings are low positively barred from entering the university. However, experience accumulated over several years has shown that few students with low ratings will insist on a university course. If, in the face of all the facts, such students enter the university, a conference is sought with the parents at once, so that they may know something of the handicaps under which their son or daughter is laboring. This advice is almost uniformly welcomed by the parents and it often saves much grief later.

Perhaps the most significant thing about the Minnesota movement for testing high school seniors is that all of the educational forces of the state, the public schools, the private colleges, and the state university, are engaged in a gigantic cooperative enterprise whose sole purpose is that of advising high school seniors as to whether they should or should not go to college. Here is a selective agency at work which still possesses all the elements of human sympathy. It does not hold up an absolutely invariable and unmodifiable stop-and-go sign. It does not say, "Thus far you may go, beyond you shall not go." It recognizes that human judgment may err, that statistics may lie. Above all it recognizes that great American principle — the right to try — knowing full well that industry sometimes succeeds even when high intelligence is wanting. And still the plan works; students of higher and higher ability are coming to college, some of little or less ability still come, but not all those of superior ability find it possible to come. The thing about it all that appeals to me is that we have here a democratic method, a democratic experiment in democracy, if you please, that does not close the doors of opportunity to the aspiring slow students but encourages those of greater talents to seek training for leadership in increasing numbers.

After students are admitted, the university is at once faced with the responsibility of providing them with the most effective educational conditions. Aside from the usual physical facilities and curricular offerings which any student body has a right to expect, the university is doing certain things for the purpose of increasing its educational effectiveness that are more or less unusual.

The first of these is the attention it is giving to the individual student. With the physical, intellectual, and emotional examination of students, the information obtained from the vocational and educational advisers, the student counselors, the psychiatrist, the personnel committee and the deans of men and of women, we actually know more about our students today than at any other time in the history of the university.

There is still talk, to be sure, about the loss a student sustains in failing to come into more intimate personal contact with the staff. This is one of the traditional educational myths. Most of us never enjoyed that intimate personal contact when we were in college. We didn't want it. I had college instructors that I wouldn't have walked across the street to shake hands with. I had others whom I respected and revered and I established contacts with them. The situation in university circles today is not essentially different in this respect from what it was then. Twenty and thirty years from now, this present student body will be pointing back to the successors of William Watts Folwell, Dr. Northrop, Maria Sanford, Dean Eddy, Professor Pattee.

But we know more about the students than they

did. We say it reverently and without boast. The agencies we have set up contribute through scientifically acquired knowledge and technique to a system of intelligent advising for individual students.

A second respect in which the University of Minnesota is contributing to improved educational conditions is in the constant and continuing study of its problems. A committee on university research, consisting of men from each of the several colleges of the university, was established a few years ago. This committee has now completed a number of studies of supreme importance to the university.

It has discovered, for example, that the size of class is no measure of the achievement of students. The effect of this study has been revolutionary in college circles in America.

It has discovered that students with the best scholastic records are in general the students who participate most actively in extra-curricular activities. This conclusion was most astonishing to those dwellers in Academe who assume that students should be thin-chested, bespectacled, confirmed bookworms.

It has discovered that the method employed in teaching science, whether it be the lecture, the question and answer, the demonstration method, or some combination of these, does not seem to make very much difference.

It has discovered that students who have had high

school physics have no distinct advantage in college physics over students who have had no physics.

It has discovered that certain prerequisites in certain fields have almost no value in the fields for which they are supposed to prepare.

It has discovered that the most important causes of student mortality are ill health and lack of money and that the most important cause of failure in college is lack of will power or character.

These are only a few of the significant conclusions that this committee has reached. It can be safely said, I believe, that no university in America is doing more than the University of Minnesota in studying its internal problems of educational procedure. This movement has just begun. In the not distant future we shall know enough to organize and administer our colleges scientifically both as to their offerings and as to their techniques.

Here at Minnesota we are now engaged in another study of vast significance. It is a study which grows out of the fact that knowledge has been so split and differentiated that it is now practically impossible for one to obtain a comprehensive understanding of any field of human learning. With the departmental organization that now exists, it is difficult for one to obtain a liberal education. Even the specialists, who have been caught in the net of their specialisms, have begun to recognize this fatal educational weakness and are demanding an increasing amount of training of a general nature. Law, medical, and engineering faculties are supplementing their ranks with professors from allied and even from remote fields to fill the gaps that exist in their programs. Gradually and somewhat painfully the social order has come to the conclusion that men who are sharpened to a point must have broad bases if the broader interests of human welfare are to be considered. The attenuation of human knowledge into unrelated lines is one of the causes, if not the chief cause, of educational unrest. Minnesota has recognized this and she has created a committee whose definite purpose is to make recommendations with a view to simplifying the educational program and effecting a coordination of the offerings in such a manner as to insure more general training for those expecting to enter the various specialties. If through education men can be made more cosmopolitan in their views, more catholic in their sympathies, more humanitarian and less self-centered in their opinions, the University of Minnesota should be among the leaders in achieving such ends.

Perhaps mention should also be made of the committee of experts that is studying the place of physical education and athletics in the university program. This committee is composed of as able a group of disinterested experts as it was possible to obtain. It is not possible to predict what the report will be. But that it is time such a study be made, no one familiar with the problem will deny. Everywhere, from the Atlantic to the Pacific and from Canada to the Gulf, grave concern is being manifested over the increasing amount of public attention college athletics, especially football, is receiving. There are those in college circles who believe in the game, who desire to preserve it and its benefits, but who view with alarm attempts to exalt it beyond the educational function and work of the institutions they represent. A constructive plan, assigning to physical education and athletics their proper places in a sound educational program, will, I am convinced, eventually commend itself to all those interested in the genuine welfare of their university. And here again it is the hope of the university officials that Minnesota may be counted among the leaders.

There is one more matter in which we are deeply interested at Minnesota and to which I wish to call your attention before this paper is brought to a close. Most of us are aware that we are living in a new world. Science and machines have made it. We are in danger of being more interested in products than in personalities, in individuals than in human beings. With mass production, standardization of articles, combinations and mergers of capital, thousands of our youth are, through long and indefinite apprenticeships, in danger of developing routine or high-grade clerical types of mind.

EDUCATIONAL TRENDS

With a world changing almost overnight, with machinery being replaced every few years, with science venturing into unknown realms and revealing hidden secrets of vast importance, education must be continuous even for adults or they will soon lose step in the march of human progress. The desire to keep the road to promotion open, on the one hand, and to provide general training of a liberalizing character for everyone, regardless of age, was never so imperative as now. Hence the movement for adult education. Minnesota is participating in the study of this movement. She has placed three members of her staff on part time and assigned to them the problem of studying the adult educational agencies of the state with the hope that there may eventuate a constructive program, state-wide in scope and fundamental in importance. Can anyone really picture what would happen to a state if all its various agencies were united in a great cooperative undertaking designed to promote the common welfare through the continuing education of all the people?

Perhaps it may be said that this is too vast a picture for any one vision; we may even be accused of being visionary and utopian in suggesting it. But it is my settled conviction that democracy is nothing but a process of continuous education. To halt the process will mean the disintegration of democracy. Not only is it necessary if the institutions of democracy are to survive, but it is necessary also if unemployment and dependent old age are not to become greater and greater social and economic burdens.

Already I have talked far beyond what I intended to say when I began this paper and I have said nothing about the use of the radio in education, nothing about the programs in fundamental research which the university is encouraging, and nothing about money to carry on the work of the university. I have said nothing about money for the simple reason that sooner or later the idealism of the people of the state will center upon the work of the university, and funds from both private and state sources will be supplied in increasing abundance. Once the people begin to think of the real work of the university, once they recognize how important it is to economic progress and to social welfare, they will see that the emphasis is put where the emphasis belongs, and the funds will be supplied.

Already the university has a national and an international reputation. Today she ranks fifth among the universities of America in the number of foreign students who have come here for advanced study. This week we have upon the campus two distinguished men from Italy, two from Russia, one from Germany, one from Holland, two from England, who have come here to lecture. Within the past few weeks members of her staff have been invited to perform expert service in Japan, China, Java, Liberia, Hawaii, and England.

When the day arrives that we think of the University of Minnesota primarily as a place of learning, as a community of scholars, instructing the students on the campus, exploring new fields of knowledge, and radiating its lines of influence into every part of the state, then the university will begin to dwell in a true university atmosphere. When students dwell on studentship, professors on teaching and research, alumni on the educational traditions, and citizens on the humanities and the achievements of science rather than on the size of the economic rewards of life, then the university of which Dr. Folwell dreamed, and which we through all these years have tried to fashion, will come into being.

IX

ADULT EDUCATION

*An address delivered before the Department of
Superintendence of the National Education
Association, Detroit, February 25, 1931*

I N THIS paper I propose to confine myself
to a single aspect of the adult education
movement. I propose to discuss it as a means
of solving the problem of unemployment. Nothing
exceeds this in importance just now. The world is
more deeply concerned with it than it is with any
other single issue. Thousands of panaceas are being
offered for the restoration of economic prosperity and
the reduction of unemployment. There is no good
reason why the schoolmaster should not present his;
it cannot be more visionary than those presented by
the captains of finance and industry.

Here we are in the midst of the direst economic de-
bacle the world has ever witnessed. It reaches around
the world; it touches all people and affects life on
every level. In the United States we are faced with
an unparalleled record of business and bank failures.
Millions are unemployed. Governmental and charit-

able agencies are called upon to relieve economic and social conditions.

Our leaders stand before us helpless, advocating for the most part a laissez faire policy. They maintain that if things are left alone they will right themselves soon and that when they have once adjusted themselves we shall enter upon a period of permanent prosperity. They would have us believe that panics will cure themselves. Intelligence, courage, and common sense are to be displaced by optimistic blindness. All this, I think, means that we are suffering from a helpless and misguided leadership. The present disaster and all others like it are an indictment of our civilization. When poverty and misery and unemployment stalk abroad in the midst of plenty, the time has come for an accounting of the leadership that produces such conditions. With our whole economic structure and the institutions depending upon it, including education, in distress, it is time that we began to look for causes and to seek remedies. For this economic depression is not the last one that will occur; indeed, unless something in the nature of a permanent solution is found, depressions will come with increasing frequency and increasing momentum. It is clear that we have a job to do and that it must be done with foresight and intelligence. Fitful spurts of artificial prosperity only involve us the more deeply in the approaching maelstroms of tomorrow.

But what contribution can adult education make to this problem? A recent survey in Minneapolis, St. Paul, and Duluth showed that approximately 50 per cent of the unemployed are forty-five years of age and over. Many have lost out because of technological conditions resulting from the introduction of machinery; others are of the house-to-house salesman type for whom there is no longer any need; others have been dropped to reduce overhead when mergers were effected; still others have been displaced by younger men at less salary. What shall we do with this increasing army of men and of women for whom the tide of life is beginning to ebb? Shall we assume that the number must increase and that we must care for them with a government dole? Shall we assume that this situation is merely an inevitable phase of the struggle for progress and that nothing can be done about it? The first of these theories means the impoverishment of the nation and the permanent pauperization of millions of self-respecting persons who are willing to work, while the conclusion that increasing unemployment is a necessary accompaniment of progress and that nothing should be done about it, spells communism in the long run.

Recently I listened to a long discussion of this problem by two men prominent in the banking interests of a midwestern city. The general drift of the conversation was that we have always had unemployed; why worry about them? If they had saved as they should when they had employment, they would not now be objects of charity. Give them as little as possible, these men said; let them suffer; that is the only way that they and their kind will ever learn the lessons they need to know.

These bankers were ignoring one of the simplest and most elemental considerations of economics, which is that no financial depression can ever be solved by perpetuating poverty. They failed to remember that the things men want are protection for their homes, security of position, education for their children, and all the benefits and comforts that science can contribute to their living. These things they are willing to work for; these things they will have even if they have to obtain them in some new way. Communism in its various forms will not be held at bay by negative actions and attempts at government regulation; instead there must be positive action and constructive programs if we are to be spared the consequences of outbreaks of violence. Despair expresses itself in desperate acts. The governments of the world today are at the crossroads. We delude ourselves with the pleasant thought that our own government is so secure that nothing can happen to it, but this is merely a delusion.

In the midst of such a crisis what shall we do? What can we do? Some say, give pensions to the aged and the unemployed. Certainly pensions for the old would be better in every way than doles for the young.

But there is something else that may be tried, and now I come to the point I have had in mind to make. There is no good reason why civilization should not continue to advance; there is no reason why more and more wealth should not be produced; there is no reason why human wants should not be multiplied. More and more, industry and business must provide for those who have been employed long enough to be regarded as permanent employees. But many types of business and of industry will disappear and others will arise to take their places. There must be a constant inventory of the trends in industry and in business. This is one of the things we have been attempting to do for our region at the University of Minnesota. We have made a study of 450 business establishments. We can tell you which ones are on the up grade and which ones are on the down grade. We are of the opinion that we know which will pass out of existence in the next few years, which will hold their own, and which will become stronger. This is valuable information for the young person about to enter upon a career; it is equally valuable for those men and women now in the employ of decadent industries who will soon be tramping the streets looking hunger in the face unless something constructive is done.

And that is what our university proposes to undertake. We have begun a careful analysis, not of business trends merely, but of the social, economic, and educational background of the unemployed. We are giving informational, intelligence, and vocational tests to thousands of such persons. We shall select the casuals from the capables, the stupid and ignorant from the intelligent, the unambitious from the ambitious, those who do not want to work from those who are willing to work.

Then in cooperation with the officials of the state and of the three largest cities of the state the university proposes to inaugurate an educational program for those who are capable of profiting by training. This intensive program will be carried on in the closest cooperation with the placement agencies of the state and of the cities. We are gathering together the best students the country affords in the vocational, sociological, and economic fields to assist in mapping out the program and to supervise it while it is under way. We propose to carry this on for two years at least. During that time we hope to show that it is possible to mitigate the problem of unemployment in one area. To put it the other way round, we expect to increase the number of employed, and in so doing to stage for the rest of the country what will in effect be a demonstration of a partial solution of the problem of unemployment. And we believe that the rest of the country can do and should do what we are doing or think we shall be able to do.

There are, to be sure, those in our midst who say

that we should be spending more on feeding the hungry and less on studying the problem. They are the men who have helped to produce the present disaster. They smile at the impractical dreams of the schoolmaster and continue to spread their propaganda. They are the men who send humanity chasing after ever disappearing and constantly recurring economic rainbows. And the pitiful thing about it all is that many of the sufferers in our present grim world tragedy continue to follow blindly after them. But there are others, and I hope increasing millions, who are thinking of preserving their self-respect, the self-respect of their families, and the institutions of their forbears.

Whether a university can make use of adult education to renew hope among despairing thousands remains to be demonstrated. There seems to be no good reason why it should stand helpless along with the economic leadership that has produced world calamity. Others may seek to prevent the recurrence of the plague that menaces us by enacting legislation, by advocating fewer hours of labor a day, fewer days of work a week, higher wages, and the purchase of more of the goods of life without increasing their cost. But education and educational institutions may do much, by the study and use of adult education, to drive fear and terror from the hearts of those who are caught in the network of industry and do not know how to extricate themselves.

X

FLEXNER AND THE STATE UNIVERSITY

*A paper published in the Journal of Higher
Education, October, 1931*

NO STATE university lives in the paradise which Mr. Flexner has created. Every state university is guilty to a greater or less extent of all of the indiscretions to which he alludes. As one charged with the responsibility of administering a state university, I come from reading Mr. Flexner's book with conflicting opinions and impressions. I find myself at one time in complete agreement with many of his fundamental theses, at other times at variance with the spirit of his discussion and with the philosophy he enunciates in defining what universities should be.

No one, so it seems to me, can question his statement that a university is an expression of the age in which it exists, nor can anyone take issue with the thesis that universities should not be expected to conform to a single pattern. In other words, universities are the products of social evolution. They differ as to nature, in time, national temperament, and the spirit and problems of the age. And again, one finds himself in complete agreement with Mr. Flexner when he says that universities should not be weather vanes, responsive to every variation of popular whim. Their aims and purposes and functions reach beyond the demands and caprices of the moment.

Mr. Flexner makes these principles still more concrete when he says that "we should see to it somehow that in appropriate ways scholars and scientists would be conscious of four major concerns: the conservation of knowledge and ideas; the interpretation of knowledge and ideas; the search for truth; the training of students who will practice and 'carry on.'" (*Universities: American, English, German*, p. 6.)

He maintains that the conservation of knowledge, important though it may be, is nevertheless incidental to the other three purposes. A university, in his opinion, should be less interested in reconstructing the past than it is in understanding the present and in revealing the future. It should be more concerned in discovering the truth than in using it. It should understand and interpret the world and yet not be of it. A university should be a place characterized largely, if not chiefly, by a spirit of creative and critical inquiry. This inquiry should not be confined to the fields of science. It should interest itself in humanism in all its aspects. It does not seem to me that anyone can take exception to any of these theses.

Then, too, it must be admitted, as Mr. Flexner states, that all college work is not of equal value, although the present system of credits and honor points may create the impression that it is. It must also be acknowledged that there is much superficial work done in colleges, that courses have at times been attenuated to the point of transparency, and that some theses accepted for advanced degrees prove the obvious.

I believe that Mr. Flexner is right in maintaining that we are disposed sometimes to overemphasize the vocational point of view in much of the work done in university circles. Insufficient emphasis is given to fundamentals and to that broader and richer background upon which the specialties should be based. The more an individual is sharpened to a point, the broader the base should be. The greater the degree of specialization, the richer the background should be.

After I have listed all of the principles with which I find myself in substantial agreement, however, I am still disposed to differ from Mr. Flexner in two respects: I do not believe that the work of the universities is so bad as one would infer from reading his book; and, second, I believe that the university which he longs for does not exist, never has existed, and never will exist. Certainly no state university can, nor is it ambitious to dwell in the realm of intellectual exclusiveness. Being earthly, these institutions to some extent smack of the earth. Being creatures of democracy, they possess the strengths and weaknesses that democratic human institutions ordinarily have.

Most state universities include in their offerings subjects which Mr. Flexner abhors, or at any rate would eliminate from their programs. They have schools of journalism, of home economics, of business administration, of library science, of pharmacy, and of agriculture, and they maintain extension departments; in addition, their service functions bulk large in their programs. Mr. Flexner is of the opinion that the introduction of such work as a part of a university program should be resisted.

What is included in the program of a university is not altogether a matter of what some one person thinks. Resistance to popular pressure may be a fine and noble thing, but carried too far the individual may become a martyr to his exclusive thinking, and the institution he hopes to save may become impotent by its very isolation.

Mr. Flexner objects to the presence in a university program of such courses as those mentioned above on the ground that they lower standards and thus adulterate and dilute the "cultural" work. In other words, the presence of these "substitutes for culture" has a demoralizing effect upon the college by lowering its dignity. Mr. Flexner does not contend that such work is not socially valuable or that it should not be offered, but he inveighs against its being offered in universities.

Mr. Flexner maintains somewhat vigorously that a university should undertake to understand the movements and changes that are constantly occurring in our social order, but if I understand him correctly, it should not be concerned with the training of individuals for the practical vocations arising out of these changes. And yet, so it seems to me, the entire history of university education has been in the direction of greater practicality. Almost every expansion of the curriculum has arisen out of some social need. The "liberal" studies of each age have been the practical studies of that age. These studies differ from age to age. New studies have come in because new needs have arisen, and old ones have disappeared when old needs have become obsolete. Universities will teach what the people want. A university that fits for nothing, that lays only broad bases with no objectives in view, that has no ideal but that of understanding and interpreting knowledge, searching for truth, and training others who are to understand and interpret knowledge and search for truth, will, I am sorry to say, find it rather hard sledding in this practical world of ours. Furthermore, it is a fact that students who know what they want are coming to college in increasing numbers. Universities, certainly state universities, are not merely places for the living of an intellectual life; they are definitely designed and maintained to train practitioners for higher levels of service.

State universities are peculiarly the products of American democracy. The philosophy which accounts for their origin and in which they are still rooted is powerful and impelling. In referring to their functions and responsibilities, President William Allan Neilson puts the point well:

"In the western states the university is the great central source of expert knowledge of all kinds, and it is open to discussion whether it can define and limit its functions as rigidly as Mr. Flexner would have it do. The knowledge of fact and theory in agricultural, economic, and domestic fields that is called for by the people of a state, is theirs by right if they are willing to pay for it, and the state university with its complex organization, its varieties of research, its academic and non-academic methods of instruction, is the institution which has grown up to meet these needs. It may well be that the various divisions of the university would do their work better if they were separated; but this is a matter of organization and terminology. The professors of classics are not seriously disturbed in their philological labors because a colleague in the agricultural department gives advice to farmers on the best breeds of cattle for milk or beef, though the president (for whom Mr. Flexner has a very modified respect) might welcome a simplification of his functions." ("Town and Gown Today," *Journal of Adult Education*, April, 1931.)

It would be interesting, I think, for those persons who are of the opinion that learning may be concentrated in a few semi-private institutions of a prestige character, to note the changes that have taken place in recent years in the location of men of science and scholarship, and also to check the contributions to science and scholarship which have been made by men associated with state institutions as compared with those by men associated with private institutions. It would be discovered that there has been an astonishing drift of men of science and scholarship to state institutions. In my opinion, this is one of the most hopeful things that is happening in the interest of democracy. I believe that such men should be fairly well scattered throughout the entire nation rather than concentrated at a few places. If science is to flourish, and its applications to receive fair consideration, if scientists and scholars are to perpetuate their own kind, and if the leavening influence of scientific effort and scholarship is to permeate society in general, then a movement for the distribution of such leaders of thought to many centers of learning is a movement in the right direction.

State universities are peculiarly sensitive to change; they are in intimate contact with life. It is impossible for them to live in the past or in some intellectual empyrean. They are, as Mr. Kinley, former president of the University of Illinois, has said, "the developmental arm of the state." And as President Chase declared in his inaugural address: "Like every other sort of organization, it [the state university] realizes its full potentialities not by attempting to take on the characteristics of any other species, but by attempting to realize to the full the possibilities of the species to which it belongs." As such it will be a place for constant experimentation with new ideas; it will be a place of intellectual ferment and stimulation; it will be a place that attempts to provide both fundamental and practical training for many different types of mind.

As public institutions, the state universities will tie themselves in more and more with the movement for adult education. They subscribe to the philosophy that democracy in the long run is nothing but a process of continuous education. They will undertake to raise the cultural level of all of the people as well as the cultural level of those who are to assume leadership among the people. Cultural levels are something that cannot be imposed; they must arise out of the needs of the people themselves. And culture, it may be added, is the most important by-product of any program of studies.

No matter what any of us may think, state universities will continue to be peculiarly American. If new needs arise they will respond to them willingly. If new types of vocational and professional training are required they will provide them. If through the dissemination of information and other forms of service they can improve the standard of living, increase the culture, enjoyment, and happiness of the people, they will not shrink from such opportunities. And while they are doing these things they will give increasing attention to their teaching and research responsibilities.

Although I find it difficult to subscribe to Mr. Flexner's philosophy throughout, nevertheless I believe that his is the most stimulating and thoughtful book in the field of university education that has appeared since Cardinal Newman's.

XI

EDUCATION AND THE DEPRESSION

An address delivered during Schoolmen's Week,
University of Minnesota, March 25, 1932

T HE problems growing out of the current issues of our economic life are imperiously crying out for solution. Obviously American democracy is faced now as never before with the necessity of outlining and pursuing programs far in the future. The alternative is to muddle along in the fervent hope that time and some fortuitous combination of circumstances will solve our problems for us. The first is the high choice of intelligence and courage; the second is the paltering recourse of ignorance, sloth, and fear.

The problems call for a reappraisal of every phase of our governmental and institutional relations. They are a challenge to thinking people in every walk of life. In the consideration of them, self-interest should be entirely forgotten. Everyone must be deeply concerned that frenzied, unreasoned appeals be replaced by constructive programs looking to the future. No

164

broken-down and patched-up political and social and economic arrangement will provide a lasting remedy for our present ills. If we follow this path, the system will break again, bringing greater human ruin in its train the next time.

Naturally I am interested in the relation of the schools to the readjustments with which we are faced. I think I can, and I certainly hope I have been able to dissociate myself far enough from the particular position I hold to consider without prejudice this phase of the general problem in relation to public welfare. On the other hand, an experience with schools extending over forty years may make me particularly sensible to their worth. What I am about to say is naturally and properly colored by such an experience but I assure you it is not controlled by it nor by the special institutional interests which are normally my responsibility. These are not normal times. The standard by which we must judge utterances and policies today is the single standard of a wholesome regard for public welfare.

In a crisis such as we are experiencing, the schools cannot stand apart from the other forms of organized society. They are not detached institutions. They share with all others the responsibility of aiding in the solution of the problems with which we are all confronted.

This is not the time or place to suggest a long list

of such social and economic problems. Nor can we develop here the many fields in which educators and qualified scholars and legislators and public leaders can cooperate in wise programs free from the hysteria, clamor, and subtle propaganda that often confuse the public mind at present. I must address myself chiefly to the problem that I found uppermost in my recent visit to New Zealand and the states of Australia and that I find on my return is predominating in public discussion of domestic questions in America. I mean the problem of public finance, budgets, and taxation. These important matters of public policy are in everyone's mind, and properly there. They are matters of concern to every citizen now more than ever. They are matters of concern to educators as citizens and as public trustees for the greatest social long-time investment made by taxpayers.

It is common knowledge that the depression is creating difficult financial problems in many communities and in some states. In some instances deficits actually exist. Heroic measures are being taken by citizens in these communities to balance the budgets and to carry on the work of the government and the schools. Clearly the only way to meet a deficit is to cut down on expenses or to increase taxes. Reduction of costs is the safer and more intelligent way of proceeding. Despair is added to confusion when we attempt to meet deficits by piling up a larger deficit.

EDUCATION AND THE DEPRESSION

There are, to be sure, two kinds of deficits: one is financial and the other social; one is purely a matter of balance sheets, the other is a deficit in the life and opportunities of the people.

In our desire to enrich life and to maintain its educational privileges at a high level, it is the part of wisdom for us to ask, along with the representatives of all other government beneficiaries, How much tax money do the schools need and how nearly can the people provide it? It is inherently wrong and fundamentally dishonest for any type of public institution to take disproportionate amounts of tax money — indeed, one disqualifies himself as a public servant if he asks for more than his institution needs. Needs cannot be defined in terms of mere statistics. Some imagination must be put into them; otherwise they will concern themselves with commonplace things only. Most progress has been the result of the adventurous investment of tax and private surpluses.

We may assume, I think, and with a fair degree of assurance, that the people desire that the common life of their communities and of the state shall go on, and at as high a level as they can consistently support it. The thing that we are particularly anxious about is that the humanitarian and educational institutions shall play the part they are capable of in meeting the present crisis and that they may not become the victims of an unreasoned movement for retrenchment.

167

The recovery of the vigor of an institution is always slow and costly. And the greatest of the costs is to be found in the losses that both society and the institution experience during the institution's restricted life. There is little foundation for the belief that society always finds compensating returns for the damage done at such times to its humanitarian and educational institutions. If both usefulness and outlook are limited then decadence will surely set in and discouragement will take the place of hope.

It is a wise and courageous people who dare to build a democracy in which the training of youth does not fluctuate up and down with every shift of the stock market. President Graham of North Carolina, referring to this very matter, recently said: "Unwise and unnecessary curtailment of the humanitarian and educational institutions will leave empty shells to mock their former vigorous usefulness to the people."

It may be necessary — indeed, it is my personal opinion — that some adjustments in educational expenditures are natural, unavoidable. If made, they should be in terms of constructive educational reorganization rather than of destructive financial retrenchment.

There are things that can be done even in the field of education in a state like Minnesota in the way of redistricting, establishing larger units, consolidating certain agencies, and actually abandoning others. Such measures, if wisely planned, would save money and improve our educational system. Thus far the state has been unwilling to listen to a consideration of these matters because of the vested interests that localities have in them. This might be a propitious time to give consideration to all measures that promise economy without loss of efficiency.

Unfortunately the move for retrenchment has sometimes taken the form of attacks on educational and humanitarian institutions. The problems relating to education are too vital to be considered in terms of emotion or prejudice. Some retrenchment, as I said above, may be possible, but the kind I am thinking of does not involve poorer teachers, restricted programs, shortened terms, inadequately equipped schools, or reduced salaries.

The demand for lower salaries seems quite insistent, and if the things are not done that can be done, there will be no alternative but to decrease the efficiency of the schools, impair the quality of their service, and staff the schools with less competent and more poorly paid teachers. The great gains which society has made in knowledge, in the fine arts, in public and personal health, in scientific and social progress — all of which are in a way basic to our economic life and productive capacity — will at once begin to suffer. Delinquency will increase, our physical needs will be less well cared for, and our intellectual outlook will become localized and provincial.

THE STATE UNIVERSITY

Teachers are less interested, I assume, in salaries than they are in maintaining a progressively developing civilization. But this cannot be done, in my opinion, with poor schools and poor teachers. All of which means that the members of the teaching profession are faced with a challenge and an opportunity to reconstruct education without impairing its processes. Never did we have a more favorable time for making a constructive, orderly, and well integrated educational program for a state. No state has done it. The legislatures of two states — North Carolina and California — recently made provision for such programs. Members of the University of Minnesota staff have been invited to assist with the preparation of both these programs. While it is difficult for the residents of a state to study their own problems objectively, the opportunity to do so furnishes an interesting challenge for statesmanlike thinking.

We are faced with as great an issue and as genuine an opportunity as any group of schoolmasters ever faced. The issue is: Shall we surrender to the depression our spiritual vision, our intellectual outlook, and our social hopes for the youth of our generation, or hold fast with grim resolve and firm determination for the better day which constructive planning will surely bring? If we fail to embrace the opportunity, then our educational system will follow the wayward and uncertain course of the business cycles and we

170

shall be unable to plan and build, in a stable and creative way, institutions that will be unfailing sources of youthful training, of scientific and social research, and of ideas and idealism.

The philosophy to which we have held with commendable tenacity since pioneer days is that the whole life of the nation turns upon the education of the children, and the facts of the past have abundantly justified this philosophy. But this does not mean that our schools are perfect and that no changes of purpose, outlook, or program can be made in them.

Education, of course, is not the only charge against public support and private beneficence. There are those, many in fact, who maintain that charity is more essential than education. Surely no one would be so stupid as to argue for education in the face of starvation — he would feed the hungry; or for education in the presence of a dying man's thirst — he would quench the man's thirst; or for education in the face of nakedness — he would clothe the naked. Fortunately Minnesota does not face these alternatives.

We must do what the premier of Australia told the premier of New South Wales to do the other day, when the latter refused to pay the interest of the state's foreign debt. He said, "If we must choose between maintaining our credit by paying our foreign bondholders and feeding our hungry, we shall do the latter." The premier of Australia replied, "You will do both." And so shall we in Minnesota heal our sick, feed our hungry, and aid the distressed, fulfilling at the same time our obligation to provide competent teachers and an adequate educational program for our youth.

In caring for the distressed and in educating the youth, we should have a deep concern that farms and factories and savings and means of livelihood be not overtaxed. As citizens of the state with its welfare in mind, we should scrutinize expenses and revenues with the greatest care. I do not mean to imply that due consideration has not been given to these matters in the past. I am merely suggesting that we make them the object of special consideration at this time. Schoolmasters are not politicians. They, of all classes, can afford to apply the cold light of reason rather than the white heat of emotion to questions of taxation.

There is danger, if I am correctly informed, that some communities and even some states will carry their curtailments so far as to impair, if not destroy, the usefulness of their educational institutions. This only means that they are drying up the sources of their strength and future wealth. It is only through training of a high order and the stimulation of the creative imagination that a more balanced agriculture, more diversified and highly skilled industry, and more wealth of all kinds can be produced. Likewise it is through the intelligent study of facts and conditions that the solution of the unemployment and other social problems and of our domestic and foreign difficulties will come.

The issues with which we are confronted at present are so momentous and embracing as to call for a level of trained intelligence we have not hitherto provided. Hidden resources of the human mind and human spirit need to be discovered, tapped, and freed for action. Scientific information, acquired and evaluated by impartial and non-political students and critics, was never more needed. How shall we discover these resources and acquire this information? Not by drifting or supinely waiting with expectant hope. We must create our way from the depression into prosperity, from fear to courage, from planlessness to purposefulness.

If there must be a curtailment of intellectual opportunity then it should be as temporary as possible, for in the meantime research essential to welfare and progress will suffer. Indeed, it will practically cease if the curtailment means an increased load for those engaged in teaching. One cannot refrain from saying that at such a critical time there should be a careful reweighing of values. The March, 1932, issue of the *National Sphere* contains this statement:

"The automobile industry says that the cost of operating a small pleasure automobile is 6.43 cents a mile, and that the average number of miles such a car runs in a year is 11,000, so that the annual cost of up-keep of a small car is $707.30. There are, in round numbers, 23,000,000 pleasure cars registered in the United States. The estimated cost of operating them all, therefore, is in excess of $16,000,000,000 a year.

"The government's latest figures show that the total gross farm income is $6,920,000,000. The gross cost of education, including all schools, is $3,200,000,000 a year. One of the trade papers estimates that the total cost of all buildings in the United States, in 1931, was $4,312,000,000. The figures seem to indicate that the cost of upkeep for pleasure automobiles, including depreciation, is substantially greater than the gross farm income plus the total cost of education plus the total cost of buildings."

Dr. Julius Klein, assistant secretary of commerce, is authority for the statement that the greatest single line of expenditure made by residents of our impor-tant farming states is the automobile. We spend more for its maintenance and operation than we spend for food, clothing, or shelter. It would be possible, of course, to show that we are still spending literally bil-lions for nonessentials and luxuries.

We may well ask: Is it better to continue heavy expenditures of this character or to provide more edu-cation for children who will find the ways of pro-viding improvements for their generation? Which is better, one may ask, to incur debts for buildings, roads, and other enterprises to be paid for by the next generation, or to provide a more competent educational system and finer humanitarian agencies? Are there those who maintain that an inadequately equipped school, taught by a poorly trained, half-competent teacher — a cheap school — can produce anything but cheap education?

In periods of depression it is always easy to strike quickly and effectively at the welfare and educational agencies for the simple reason that public interest in them is so widely diffused. Then, too, those responsible for their administration are frequently regarded as dreamers and special advocates, thus minimizing the effectiveness of their appeals.

Two things seem perfectly clear and reasonable to me: The first is that every agency and institution of the state deriving any or all of its funds from the state treasury should join with the state in maintaining its credit and in balancing its budget. The second is that no state institution should spend a state's dollar that it would not spend in case the institution were the private property of the administration.

The converse of these two things seems equally clear and reasonable. It is that a state, in balancing its budget and in maintaining its credit, should proceed in a constructive manner so as not to cripple those agencies that are essential to its growth and economic welfare. No state can expect a revival of its economic life and a renascence of the human spirit – no state can expect life and life more abundantly – by underfeeding the forces of growth and idealism. Budget-making in a depression becomes a test of what we really believe in.

The interests of a state are served best by a thoroughly competent and efficient school system. We may be able to restrict its resources for a brief time without seriously impairing it, but there is danger even then that we shall not be buying the equipment the schools need, that the teachers will be carrying too heavy a load, that the instruction will suffer and the educational advancement of children will be retarded. Then, too, in such circumstances it will be difficult to maintain the high professional spirit among the teachers that we have labored for fifty years to develop.

Schools are not like departments of state, and should not be so regarded or administered. In spite of depressions the children keep on coming. There is no shortage of youth. For years now we have been struggling to give them increasingly superior advantages on the ground that more and better training is needed by each succeeding generation than was given the preceding generation if the problems of our complex civilization are to be met and solved.

It is popular in these days to say, "Cut out the frills, let us return to the essentials." But the frills for the most part represent our investments in idealism. To strike them unceremoniously from our school programs will leave only the barren instrumentalities of intellectual learning.

It is the frills and fads, so to speak, that have democratized education and enriched its content. Under the influence of the compulsory education laws every type of human mind comes to school. To assume that the old curriculum with its three *R*'s and its emphasis upon Latin and mathematics in the upper schools would appeal to the variety of human minds now found in the school is to display an abysmal ignorance of human nature. The fads and frills came in under the pressure of impressive social sanctions. They came in because of the demand for a richer training adapted as far as possible to the needs and capacities of every type of human mind.

The expressive subjects have gradually taken their place alongside the reflective subjects; the old, stiff, formal kind of education has been superseded by a more active and effective kind. The presence of these new subjects in the curriculum is the true test of the school's socializing power. To eliminate them will mean that we shall lose the greatest gains that have been made in education in the last fifty years. The animating spirit of the schools will be destroyed — they will once again become wooden and listless. The common school will no longer be the hope of the country.

THE STATE UNIVERSITY

If it is important that a commonwealth preserve the integrity of its public schools, it is equally, many would say that it is doubly, important that it watch with fostering care over its higher schools. These institutions, to be sure, must be responsive to changing conditions and willing to bear their fair share of the burden in any crisis. These institutions must carry on the researches and supply the trained leadership for tomorrow. In general, the members of their staffs have made heavy sacrifices extending over many years in the interest of scholarship, science, and human progress.

One does not become a professor before middle life. Men who chose the academic life as a career did so with no thought of a fortune in mind. They knew they would be working at a financial loss when business conditions were good; they knew there would be no adjustment of their salaries to rising markets. Never once in all their experience did they expect that fortune would come to them because of an upward swing of the market. Even now in the present crisis, the facts show that their incomes coincide almost exactly with the curve of the cost of living. For twenty years they have been living on deflated incomes, struggling as best they could to advance learning and to promote scholarship. In so far as they were affected by economic motives they chose teaching for two reasons, namely, the tradition that men in professional positions have permanency of tenure and the assurance of continuity of employment and income without regard to business cycles. A lower income than most of them would have earned in other professions or business was cheerfully accepted because of security of tenure and salary. They were willing to devote themselves to the intellectual life and to social progress in the faith that these assurances would be kept. They took, so to speak, the vows of a self-denying profession for the benefit of youth and human progress.

Of course times may come, conditions may arise, just as they did during the World War, when the staffs of the higher institutions of learning will regard it as their patriotic duty to relinquish or to hold in abeyance their ideals. They will do their larger duty then. History has shown, however, when such crises arise and the university and college staffs respond to them, that the social gains are always accompanied by heavy corresponding losses. One always needs to weigh the losses as well as the gains. To bring the teaching staff of any level of education nearer to the level of subsistence means fewer books, fewer magazines, less science, less progress, a weakened professional interest, and it makes the profession itself less attractive. When such a misfortune is visited upon the higher institutions it must inevitably take years to restore their efficiency, to revive their scholarship, and to re-engage them in research.

We cannot pinch our way through to prosperity; nor can we pay the long-running debts that have been incurred without developing the creative power of the people. The economic condition of our people must be made safe. Debts must be paid, with interest. Budgets must be balanced. Needs that are not imperatively necessary must be postponed. Let us do these things, if possible, by building up, not by tearing down. This is the surest and safest way of paying our debts, of vanquishing poverty, and of restoring hope.

A wise business people who have regard for their own interests and who cherish what they owe their children will, through all and in spite of the winds of frenzied finance, keep constantly at a high level the intellectual and spiritual resources of their life and power. It is in the course of great business depressions that we test our intelligence and inventory our convictions. To lower the quality of life for which improvements have been made and which has been achieved after heroic struggles by our less prosperous forefathers would be a betrayal of the great sacrifices which animated and directed the life and thought, the dreams and hopes of these pioneers.

It is of the highest importance that the American people reassert their faith in these fundamental matters at this time. In curtailing our budgets we must not lose our democracy. Already dictatorships and communism and special interests have encroached upon the ideals and processes of democracy in other parts of the world. And we are not without signs that some of these forces are stalking boldly in the open in America. It would be an irreparable misfortune if we sacrificed both democracy and our children in the name of economy.

For more than three hundred years American democracy has planted its roots in one territorial frontier after another. Its springs, if I may change the figure, were kept flowing, fresh and open. But now the last territorial frontier is gone. Today the new frontiers are found in the problems arising out of political, social, and economic life. The springs which will give us sustaining strength for the solution of these problems are found in the schools from the primary grades to the university. If they are not found there, then they are found nowhere. The only way we have of making progress is through education. It is the only sure guarantee of civilization. If we fail there, we fail everywhere.

We should improve the forms of progress, correct the neglect of public responsibility, refuse to fall prey to the mechanical appliances of civilization, establish new and enduring international relations, insist upon universal peace and disarmament, study our domestic problems, spend nothing unwisely — but hold fast to the thought of providing as generously as possible for the spiritual growth and capacity of every human being in the community. We may discover that the chief joy and consolation of the poor man is the opportunity the schools afford his children. Instead of a concentration of privileges, there is still much to be said for a wider distribution of opportunities. Whatever we find it necessary to do throughout the nation, in the various commonwealths, or in our respective communities in the preparation of public budgets, careful and thoughtful consideration should be given to the needs of democracy, of equality and excellence, as well as of economy. Those who represent the schools, on the other hand, should, with equal reasonableness, limit expenditures to the paramount needs of the intellectual growth of the youth of the land and to the social and scientific requirements of the nation, making such changes in administration and policies as will, if possible, increase the effectiveness of the schools without loss of opportunity to youth and without lowering the professional standards and outlook of the teaching personnel.

THINKING IN TERMS OF TOMORROW

Phi Beta Kappa address delivered at the
University of Minnesota, May 23, 1932

PRESIDENT BUTLER of Columbia University reports a witty Englishman to have said that when Adam and Eve were wandering hand in hand through the Garden of Eden, Adam said to her, "Eve, my dear, we are living in a period of transition." If Adam was as wise as this, then he only anticipated what every intelligent man has been saying from then until now. We are always on the verge of a new era. We measure time from crisis to crisis, from deflation to deflation, from prosperity to prosperity. The course of progress is never smooth; it zig-zags up and down.

In these shiftings, human beings are forced by necessity to make millions of adjustments in order to maintain themselves. The net result of these adjustments over long stretches of time has been an improved standard of living and a broadened outlook on life. These improvements we refer to as civilization. We

usually refer to them as outgrowths or as results flowing naturally from the civilization of the past. Sometimes they are that, and again, sometimes, they are
built on the ashes of the past, with little or no apparent
connection with what has gone before.

Centuries ago there were powerful civilizations in
the Orient, whose remains can now be found by exploring in the mud and sands where they once flourished. It would be interesting and not without profit
to reflect in these days on why they did not survive.
They were powerful, able, and possessed of vast
amounts of knowledge, and yet they disappeared off
the face of the earth. Certain critics are of the opinion that they failed because their dominant philosophy
was a philosophy that worshiped the past. They were
controlled by ancestor worship and had little or no
faith in the future. Ancient civilization really ended
with them.

Not until Greece seized the idea that men and nations live by looking forward did the civilization of
the Occident begin. We accept the great philosophers,
the great poets, the great tragedians, the great orators
of Greece as our philosophers, our poets, our tragedians, our orators; we look upon its civilization as the
origin of our civilization; and all because of a moving
principle that looked for things not seen, of achievements yet to be made, of nations yet to be built, as
the guiding principle of action.

THINKING IN TERMS OF TOMORROW

To the Greeks the world in which they lived was something more than a mere changing world; it was a progressively advancing world. Change was the evidence and the opportunity for growth; lack of change was the mark of decay.

The adherents of this philosophy began to populate the world. The period of nation building began, with its inevitable conflicts and competitions. Those nations that thought in terms of tomorrow moved on; those that thought in terms of yesterday perished. Today we are still considering these two points of view, and wondering what the historians a thousand years or more from now will have to say about national ideals now dominant throughout the earth. This, I think, we may safely predict: that the future state of the human race will be decided not by arms but by ideas, not by fields of battle but by ideals, not by national isolation but by international cooperation, not by clinging to outworn and outmoded traditions and decadent philosophies but by looking for a new rainbow of promise at the close of every storm. It will be decided not by seeking cheap substitutes for brains, nor by curtailing the creative abilities of talented persons. Every time talent and ability are forced into seclusion and mediocrity comes in to replace them, demoralization begins. That nation that has courageous and forward looking leaders who dare to venture and to engage in social experimentation, that nation that has the fortitude and vision in the midst of the present world crisis to provide, encourage, and foster education for leadership, will be the nation that will write the history of the next generation.

The need of a new leadership was never more obvious. The political leaders of the world failed to avert a world war and the economic leaders have failed to avert the disaster and ruin that has engulfed the economic structure of the entire world. We are in the midst of a great revolution, vaster and more powerful than any the human race has hitherto experienced. For the time being we have lost sight of the forces and agencies that have been concerned with nation building while we are trying to establish an economic order that will insure happiness and comfort to men. We cannot achieve this highly desirable end by restoring an eighteenth-century civilization. Life is no longer simple; the wants of men are not few in number. Families have congregated in communities; communities have become states; states, nations; and nations, empires. Improved communication has annihilated distance and machinery has lifted the burden of human drudgery from the backs of men only to enslave them in a new way. The interdependence of life, of men, and of nations has become a dominant consideration in political and economic affairs. The great financial centers are reaching out their long attenuated arms into the remote corners of the earth, levying tribute upon them in new and strange ways. One cannot refrain, if he would, from experiencing a certain exhilaration and warmth of spirit when he considers the achievements of mankind.

The glow of momentary satisfaction is altogether too fleeting. We are soon reminded that we are living under a shadow, that the whole capitalistic structure of society and the institutions dependent upon it are in difficulty. The pitiful feature of the situation is that we are so devoid of intelligent planning as to the way or ways out. We have fallen prey to emotions and victims to unreasoned speech. How few there are who are building plans upon facts, who are searching for the principles that underlie and govern human action! We are not yet willing to rely upon knowledge and intelligent planning as guides for action. The world of the future will belong to the men whose understanding is based upon knowledge. Ignorance, stupidity, selfishness, greed, and planlessness are the barriers that must be surmounted if that understanding is to be effected. We need to hurry if we are to surmount them, for the sands of time are running fast and many destructive influences are at work.

No nation ever attains immortality by pursuing the material things of life. Through politics, money, and force of arms it may rule the earth, but in its strength lies its greatest danger. It is not through weakness but through misused strength that nations perish.

The historian looks behind the glory and glitter of war, the pomp and ceremony of political prestige, and the power of money for the thing that makes nations truly great. He finds it in the imponderables of life as expressed in religion, poetry, architecture, fine arts, literature. A nation that exalts and dignifies the higher things of the mind and spirit builds for itself a more permanent place in the esteem of men than a nation that exalts the material things of life.

For fear I may be misunderstood and accused of being impractical and a dreamer, I hasten to add that a national leadership that can vanquish poverty, insure the comforts of science to all men, and secure peace will, in my judgment, be contributing to the imponderables of life as truly as that leadership that concerns itself directly with the things of the spirit.

These two goals or points of view, I venture to assert, will occupy the same point on the scale of destiny, and these two types of leadership will or should be found embodied in the same men.

In America we have not yet learned how imperatively necessary it is that we think along these lines. We are still employing emotion, impulse, and quick compromise as substitutes for intelligence. We have deflated our supermen and are as yet unwilling to accept a new leadership. The old forces are still in control and the masses are apparently more helpless than ever.

THINKING IN TERMS OF TOMORROW

We have one hundred and twenty million people clamoring for relief and light but not willing as yet to use whatever knowledge may be available to save them from destruction. Their dominating motive is still an industrial and commercial motive. It is scaling down the level of living and withdrawing strength from the humanitarian and educational agencies. And yet there was never a time when knowledge — more knowledge; toleration — more toleration; cooperation — more cooperation, based on mutual understanding, were more needed than now if the great struggle in which we are engaged is to be mitigated in any fundamental respect. Nations lacking in generous aspiration and a high regard for vigorous and trained intelligence will remain inconspicuous in the history of civilization. The gods on Mount Olympus raise their eyebrows when any nation aspires to divinity by the material route alone. They rejoice and open wide the gates when the spiritual ideals of life are given their proper setting in the national scheme.

It is clear that the forces of life are engaged in a gigantic struggle; a struggle age old, to be sure, but always expressing itself in a new form. Put briefly, it is the struggle between an emergent liberalism and a decadent conservatism, between the forces of change and those of the status quo — a struggle for existence and growth. The intensity of this struggle is registered on every hand. The eternal battle between these two forces is never ended. It flares up, becomes more intense at times, and then dies down for a period. It exhibits itself in the life of every institution. We have it in our colleges and universities. One needs only to mention the conflicting points of view that prevail on academic freedom and student government to find examples of what I mean. No matter who speaks at the university, whether conservative or liberal, no matter what is done, whether traditional or progressive, criticism is directed at the university for permitting it. And especially is this true if the subject or activity bears upon or is concerned with some social experiment. One group desires us to liberalize the minds of our students and inform them as to what is going on in the world, while the other group wishes to surround the youthful and immature minds of the students with all sorts of protecting influences. One thinks that the only cure for the ills of the world is more freedom of thought and social experiment, while the other maintains that cure lies in protection, denial, and coercion. To follow a correct path between these conflicting modes of opinion, holding steadfastly at the same time to true university purpose and traditions, is not always easy. And yet there is no other way of maintaining and insuring the integrity of our higher institutions of learning.

College and university education is society's greatest social experiment for ameliorating the struggle for existence and for training a picked lot of young men and young women for the exercise of public leadership and the effective discharge of high public responsibilities. In spite of criticism to the contrary, I believe the colleges are doing this fairly well. At any rate there is evidence of an increased recognition of the importance and necessity of such training. It is revealed in the fact that attendance has increased in recent years and that students remain in college more faithfully and for longer periods than ever before. And it is revealed in the fact that they are more serious minded today and more concerned about scholarship than they have been at any time since the war. Lectures, whether on religion, art, education, finance, or science, were never so well attended as now. These things attest more than a lingering faith in education; they are youth's unspoken search for understanding and wisdom. The young people know that education prepared and equipped a generation for the building of the greatest industrial society and commercial civilization the world has ever witnessed. They believe that education can build another civilization, one that will be more secure and better than the present, and that they will be the builders.

If a new civilization is to be built through these processes it will be because education looks to the future. If it is likely to fail in any respect, it will be because it is too conservative. I sometimes feel that we do not fit the college graduate adequately for the world in which he must live and in which the more capable are supposed to exercise a fair measure of leadership. The college graduate is, to a certain extent, the unwilling victim of an educational procedure over which he has no control, but if given the control he would be unable to extricate himself from the trap. As a result of departmentalization and of the specialization of subject matter, much of which is patterned after the industrial world, the college student does not always possess an adequate overview of the various fields of human learning, and for this reason he is lacking in that adaptability necessary for dealing successfully with the problems of the new world. Furthermore, when he gets out in the machine-made world, which man has not yet subjugated, he finds himself caught tightly in its clutches. An educational institution that thrives on specialties and a world that survives largely on repetitive activities furnish an uninspiring outlook for the college graduate. The only encouraging feature about it is that he doesn't know what is ahead of him. Can one's adaptability, initiative, and resourcefulness be brought to light, stimulated, encouraged, and still further developed through the processes of education? I believe these things can be done, but only in an institution that adapts itself to the needs of a changing world. Adherence to tradition and scorn of the currents of progress are the walls behind which the conservative hides in his effort to escape the consequences of liberalism.

I do not mean to imply by this that there is no virtue in tradition nor that the past has taught us no valuable lessons. Tradition has been the anchor that has prevented the social order from being mired in the sands or lost in the shifting currents of public opinion, and the past has revealed the futility of many ideals and programs of action. An institution that completely discards tradition, a society that abandons religion under the guise of progress, has foredoomed itself to early decay. In arguing for a look ahead I do not mean that we shall forget entirely that which has gone before. The exercise of wisdom requires time and a knowledge of circumstances.

And colleges are places maintained primarily for imparting wisdom and understanding with regard to the issues and problems of life. Sometimes both they and the lower schools fail to achieve all that they hope for. No better illustration of this can be found than the helplessness of their graduates in governmental matters. Their attitude is a laissez faire attitude, or even one of complete indifference toward the integrity and dignity of government.

One needs only to refer to the recent happenings in Congress and the campaign speeches of many of our candidates for public office to have abundant evidence of the point I am making. Statemanship all too seldom rises above the demands of some locality, and campaign oratory all too frequently is based upon a demagogic appeal. Not yet are we willing to take the facts and to use the intelligence available in the solution of our problems. We are still playing politics with human misery in our efforts to secure personal preferment. And there is no class — not even those who have benefited by college education — who dare to sound a clarion note and to stand solidly for public welfare.

There are times, I regret to say, when many of those who have been most favored neglect, defy, and willfully violate the most precious tenets and provisions of government. They even contribute to law violation, crying out at the same time against the failure of government to do their bidding. Government to them is no longer society's most powerful institution, designed and maintained with public good as its dominating motive; on the contrary, it represents localized and provincial points of view. It has become weak and vacillating because it lacks intelligent support from the electorate. The result is that representative government everywhere is on trial. Have we the courage, the necessary intelligence, and the strength of character to lift it out of the slough of ineptitude and abandon that it has fallen into? No graver problem, I dare say, faces the present group of graduates.

THINKING IN TERMS OF TOMORROW

My recent experiences in visiting the universities of New Zealand and Australia, and what I know of many European universities, lead me to the conclusion that we may not be so thorough and rigid in our intellectual training as we should be. By softening it in response to all sorts of pressures from parents, students, and the public, we have weakened its effectiveness. True, we teach the students many facts, but we have failed, to some extent at least, to teach them how to organize, classify, infer, test, think. The students are of the opinion that they possess the necessary bases for independent thought and independent action. They soon discover, after they leave us, that the world is not to be opened with the instruments that they possess. Marks and grades are not necessarily indications of the ability to think. One thinks only when he has a problem, he has a problem only when he is curious about something. Curiosity sends him on the search of facts and ideas. The problems of life were never more onerous, never more grave or more difficult; never was there more need for — and never was there less, so it seems to me — thought and action based on facts, in government and business.

I sometimes wonder whether we send our graduates away from us with as much of a flair to achieve something as we should. To be sure there are as many exceptions to this as there are to the other statements I have just made, but by and large the statements hold true. But it is a fact that we have been concerned more with the intellects of our students and less with their emotions, and in so doing have failed to cultivate impelling appreciations. Appreciation based upon understanding is the highest type of appreciation, but there is such a thing as understanding without appreciation. The same subject matter may be taught by two persons: one will produce saints; the other, sinners. The same subject matter taught by two persons will produce enthusiasm and intellectual curiosity in the one case and indifference and complacency in the other. One of the time-honored traditions of colleges and universities is that they shall not send out their graduates as advocates of any dogma, creed, or theory. With that doctrine I fully agree. On the other hand, they and particularly those who belong to the intellectual elect should go from us with a great emotional urge to continue to learn, to understand, to achieve, and to foster and encourage the arts and humanities in every form.

Someone said not long ago that what America needs is a new fairy tale. One reason, the critics say, for some of the ineffectiveness of education is that we have no philosophy controlling conduct and action except the philosophy that there shall be no philosophy. We need a new controlling philosophy for our feelings and ideas to cluster around. We need a new imponderable to displace despair and discouragement with hope and optimism. The fairy tale which will accomplish this must be a practical fairy tale, the imponderable must be attainable. The Argonauts who go in quest of this fairy tale cannot be mythical persons. If they are to indoctrinate their followers, and they must if civilization is to move forward, their fairy tale must be translated into constructive actions and plans; it will be because reason is supported by facts; it will be because the emotional urge is buttressed by sanity; it will be because a daring and bold leadership has entered the arena, a leadership which, like the pioneer on horseback, dares to risk being thrown only to rise and ride again. This will be a leadership that disregards self-interest and thinks in terms of public welfare rather than in terms of private interest.

The college graduate of the future will be called upon to display more creative genius and a wider range of adaptability than has yet been displayed, if life is not to be standardized and reduced to a lower level. The mechanizing influences of the machine order of civilization have already made this well-nigh impossible. Creative talents in the future must be directed more to controlling and utilizing machines than to producing them. This calls for social planning of the highest order — planning which will affect the organization of every phase of institutional life. Without such planning, tens of thousands will become veritable robots. The inauguration and adoption of such plans will not be easy, for the conservatives will remain entrenched, battling to the last ditch.

The social planning of the future will undertake to relieve poverty and distress, to invent and supply work, to remove government as far as possible from political pressure, to insure peace, to increase friendly relations at home and abroad, to advance the cause of every humanitarian and educational agency. Dreams never come true without vigorous souls to put reality into imagination. Why should we not expect, why should society not expect that such souls will be found in increasing numbers among our output? We like to think of these goals as interesting and important by-products of the educational process, but I dare say that the by-products may be socially more desirable than the direct products of education, and that they are deserving of more consideration than they receive.

There are two more respects in which the colleges need strengthening. They have failed miserably to date in teaching their students even the simplest principles of economics and finance. Either they have not known the principles themselves or they have for some unknown reason refused or failed to teach them. This hiatus should be filled so that the next generation will not become the victims of unscrupulous exploitation.

The other deficiency is that the colleges have had

no well considered program of instruction in international relationships. Never were we more provincial than now and never was there greater need of promptly establishing friendly and binding relations with foreign nations. Our students go from us with little or no knowledge of tariffs, exchange, foreign politics, treaties, or commerce. These are the men we elect to office, sometimes to high office, to enact laws and to administer government. Poorly informed, sometimes wholly untaught in these vital matters, they form unsound judgments and exercise a dangerous leadership. From this class come the demagogues who wield a pernicious power because the masses are less well informed than they are.

If what I have said thus far creates the impression that I think that the colleges and universities have failed utterly, then I have misled you. They have done acceptably well the task of their day and generation. My plea is a plea for a constant revamping and remolding of their programs and processes to fit the needs of a new day. There are certain things that seem perfectly clear. We have learned how to produce wealth but not how to use it. We have created a science only to become its slave. We live in a world of economic and political expediency. Civilization needs new tools but is still using the old ones. We have become narrow, insulated, provincial, when we need to become broader and more liberal and more cosmopolitan. We are blindly groping — trying to put the broken blocks together without knowing how. Truly Adam was right when he said, "Eve, dear, we are living in a period of transition." And transition is idealism's opportunity. Then is the time when men who know the truth should dare to speak it, and those who do not know it should try to find it.

If I have failed to congratulate the members of Phi Beta Kappa it is not that I am unmindful of their achievements but rather because of my desire to make them conscious of their responsibility. Is it too visionary to picture a new leadership arising out of the college-bred group — a leadership that has been taught in institutions that once again recognize that nation building looks to the future for things not now seen, for accomplishments not yet achieved, for victories not yet won, for aspirations not yet expressed?

THE OBLIGATION OF THE STATE
UNIVERSITY TO THE SOCIAL ORDER

An address delivered before the Conference on the Obligation of Universities to the Social Order, Hotel Waldorf-Astoria, New York City, November 15, 1932

T HE state universities originated in response to public demands and have been maintained, fostered, and encouraged all these years by the citizens of the states in which they are located. Both their origin and the sources from which they have received their support have affected their composition and the character of their activities. Growing out of and flourishing in the very soil of democracy, supported and maintained by the people, committed unequivocally to a more highly trained intelligence of the masses, believing that the road to intellectual opportunity should never be closed, maintaining a wide open door for all those who are willing to make the trial, the state universities, nevertheless, have held in common with the private universities a high sense of obligation with regard to the necessity and importance of advancing human knowledge, of promoting research, and of training those of superior gifts for especial leadership. If the presence of these two points of view in a single type of university be incompatible, then the philosophy that has animated and actuated American life from colonial days to the present time has been based upon false premises.

No state university could survive in a sheer intellectual empyrean. The state universities do not reside upon a hill. Their professors do not enjoy a cloistered life far from the marts of trade and the madding crowd. They are constantly renewing their strength by returning to the springs from which the sources of strength flow. They are constantly measuring themselves by the extent to which the life of the people whom they are serving has been changed and improved. They are constantly evaluating their effectiveness by the developing and expanding social points of view of their graduates. They share with all universities the common responsibility of advancing the cultural life of the people they serve. They do this by discovery and by adding to the sum total of human knowledge. They do this by spreading knowledge, by cultivating an appreciation of the arts, and by encouraging skill in their performance. They do this by exalting those gentler virtues of life which are seldom related to material gain. They do this by teaching the importance of reserved judgment, of tolerance of personality, and of breadth of point of view. They do this by breaking down the walls of provincialism and frowning upon pedantry. They improve the cultural life of the people by thinking about life, by attempting to understand it, and by trying to order it so as to serve mankind more faithfully and more propitiously. A university, if it be worthy of the name, no matter whether it be a state or a private university, is fundamentally and primarily dedicated to the freeing of the human spirit, to the improvement and the advancement of culture and the liberalizing of the human mind through learning and the search for knowledge.

These cultural concepts were major features in the dreams of the founders of the state universities of America. Those pioneers thought that they were building for a new day, that they were laying the foundation stones for a new civilization, a civilization which should be steeped in and influenced by the arts and the humanities on the one hand, and that should at the same time concern itself with the problems of health and economic betterment on the other. These two currents of influence came from different sources: one was from England, the other was indigenous to the American soil; one was historical and traditional, the other was concerned with the problems and issues of the new environment; one was interested in learning for its own sake, the other in learning for some useful purpose. Cherishing the past, the state universities at the same time build for the future. As impractical and idealistic as any in their reverence of knowledge, they never lose themselves so completely as to forget their pragmatic sanctions.

The state universities, as is shown by their early charters, by legislative acts, and by provisions contained in the constitutions of the states that have established such institutions, have as their first responsibility that of cherishing and transmitting the social and intellectual heritage of the race from one generation to another. It was not assumed, however, that this heritage was to be passed on unchanged. There was to be improvement in it, constant additions to it, and the transmission of it was not to be confined to those who reside upon the campus; the benefits were to flow out in every direction and to all people.

Long ago the state universities discarded for the most part the idea that their general humanizing influence was something to be confined to the humanities themselves. The expansion of the offerings in all the higher institutions of learning has been in response to the increasing complexity and differentiation of life itself. With this expansion there has come the definite recognition that culture is the most important by-product of any program of education, that its true measure is the socializing influence of the program one has been studying.

To stimulate and cultivate the intellectual and artistic interests of people in general, to socialize the practice of medicine, dentistry, law, engineering — whatever the profession or calling may be — these are high university functions and responsibilities. These responsibilities are coequal and coincident with that of educating properly those who are to occupy positions of leadership in their communities, in the state, and in the nation, as well as in their respective professions.

Closely associated with these functions the state universities have another — a service function. Doubt still lingers in the minds of some, I know, as to how far a university should go in extending its off-campus service to adults, if it does so at all. There are those who look upon this practice as a prostitution of learning and others who look upon it as a sheer and unmitigated dissipation of the intellectual life. Whatever else may be said, it nevertheless is true that the state universities have accepted and are attempting to discharge this responsibility with all the effectiveness at their command, and they are unabashed and without shame in doing it. If this be treason to the traditions of the university idea and ideal, then the state universities of America must for the most part live in a world of outcasts, for instead of decreasing their contacts with the world, they propose to increase them.

The state universities hold that there is no intellectual service too undignified for them to perform. They maintain that every time they lift the intellectual level of any class or group, they enhance the intellectual opportunities of every other class or group. They maintain that every time they teach any group or class the importance of relying upon tested information as the basis for action, they advance the cause of science. They maintain that every time they teach any class or group in society how to live better, to read more and to read more discriminatingly, to do any of the things which stimulate intellectual or aesthetic interest and effort, they thereby enlarge the group's outlook on life, make its members more cosmopolitan in their points of view, and improve their standard of living. Such services as these the state universities would not shrink from performing — indeed would seek to perform.

The chief danger inhering in university circles is that they will become intellectualized and standardized and that in consequence their pliability and usefulness as educational institutions will be diminished, if not destroyed. This does not mean that there may not be persons on any campus who work best and accomplish most when they are freest from social contacts, nor does it mean that these institutions should be so neglectful of standards and requirements as to be cheap imitations of a university. But it is certain that any university which loses step with current movements, which fails to give consideration to the sweeping changes that are occurring in every part of the world, will soon become archaic and incompetent to educate youth for the exercise of leadership.

The state universities of America today are gravely concerned about their future status and usefulness. They behold in the present crisis a movement for tax reduction affecting all institutions alike without regard to their importance. If the programs and incomes of the state universities are to fluctuate up and down with every political wind that blows, then both public welfare and the economic life of the commonwealth they are maintained to serve will suffer.

History records the important fact that whenever nations diminish their interest in and support of their universities they soon become second-rate nations. There may be other factors, to be sure, that are responsible for their decline. Spain and Portugal are nations that once enjoyed positions of world leadership – and whose universities once flourished; they are now no longer numbered among the world powers. But little nations like Denmark and Holland and Switzerland, possessing a profound respect for their universities, depending upon intelligence rather than arms for their strength, are playing an increasingly conspicuous part in international councils.

If America wishes to skip a generation in her intellectual leadership, she has only to do what I saw Russia do four years ago. Russia deprived her professors, many of whom were among the really great scholars

of Europe, of everything they needed; she exiled some
of them; she reduced her support of the universities to
a mere bagatelle. Salaries disappeared, teaching became unattractive, research impossible, and the fel-
lowships and scholarships that should have been filled
with the most talented young men were filled with
the stupid and the ignorant. To bring the teaching
staff of any level of education nearer to the level of
mere subsistence weakens the profession itself. The
social gains that we think we are acquiring by such
a procedure are always accompanied by heavy corresponding losses.

In the course of great business depressions we test
our intelligence and inventory our convictions. Each
of the preceding depressions in America was accompanied or immediately followed by a great educational revival and reawakening. It was at such times
that the foresighted pioneers of this country gathered
strength and prepared for a new day by improving
their educational system. Men recognized that the
problems of life were becoming more numerous and
more difficult and that their solution was possible only
through education. They knew that an ignorant nation would be a backward nation and that an ignorant
people would possess few of the blessings of life.

There were men during each of the preceding depressions who spent their time tinkering with this
and with that, and to some effect. There were men

who said that the only way to save the situation was
to curtail expenses, and this was done, sometimes
wisely, sometimes unwisely. There were men in those
days who struck quickly and effectively at the humanitarian and welfare institutions, crippling them in
certain localities for a generation or more. But out of
the welter of chaos and uncertainty and disappoint-
ment and unrest there emerged each time a stronger
and more profound faith in the importance and value
and necessity of American education.

Now we are in the midst of another depression.
The same forces, the same battle cries, the same demands are being made today that were formerly made
upon similar occasions. America's faith in democracy is running the gauntlet again; it is receiving another and perhaps its supreme test. If she listens to
the voices of some, America will revert to the practices of earlier days, to simpler problems and to lower
standards of living. But life will not move backward.
We shall not resign ourselves to defeat. On the contrary, we shall, I predict — indeed, there is no other
way for us — do as our fathers did; that is, inventory
the processes of education, modify and strengthen
them and build for a new day. The civilization we
enjoy was made by education. The breakdown of our
economic processes is due largely to our failure to
profit by the teachings of education. We shall not discard the instruments of growth and hope. A nation

that thinks in terms of tomorrow moves on; a nation that thinks in terms of yesterday perishes.

The future state of the nation will not be decided by seeking substitutes for brains nor by curtailing the training provided for the creative talents of youth. That nation that has courageous and forward looking leaders who dare, in the midst of the present world crisis, to provide, encourage, foster, and improve education, and especially education for leadership, will be the nation that will write the history of the next generation. The world of the future will belong to the men whose understanding is based upon knowledge.

America is making or is about to make a momentous decision. It is the decision as to what place she shall occupy among the nations of the earth in the near future. Some think this decision calls for a great army and navy; others for high tariff walls; others for national isolation; others for the breakdown of capitalism; and so on throughout a long list of proposals. But if the history of American life and tradition teaches any lesson, it is that the decision will be made in terms of the kind of education she provides for training in citizenship and for economic growth and development.

England is making the same decision. Her distress has been greater than ours. It is reported by the press that England has not reduced her appropriations for higher education. She is holding fast and with grim determination to the conviction that a competently trained intellectual leadership was never more necessary than now. She is paying the duty to intelligence that any nation must pay if it is not to be submerged by its own ignorance.

Few would venture the assertion that the problems of America are not so difficult as those of England or that those that lie ahead are not to be of increasing importance to us. Shall we wait for time and circumstance and such temporary adjustments as we are able to make to point the way to their solution? Shall we sap the sources of our intellectual strength while the struggle for existence is being intensified? Or shall we encourage the universities to use their resources to the utmost in studying the political, moral, and economic problems of the world? If the latter course be preferable, the universities must constantly be modified in the light of changing conditions and needs.

What are some of these conditions and needs? Just now we are especially conscious of the fact that the graduates of our public schools and even of our colleges and universities are helplessly ignorant about governmental matters. They know little — precious little — about the structure of government, and they are not always animated by an impelling urge to uphold, support, and advance the interests and the welfare of government.

Neither education nor public opinion has equipped

any class as yet with a knowledge of the importance of upholding the dynamic forcefulness of government. That accounts partly for the waste, greed, selfishness, lack of vision, poverty of programs, and general impotency we face in governmental matters.

Then, too, so it seems to me, we are practically a nation of economic illiterates. Certainly the great body of the American public knows little or nothing about the principles of economics. Indeed, it is doubtful whether even professors of economics have known much about these principles until recently. Our failure to teach the principles of economics is due either to our ignorance of these principles or to the fact that we were afraid to teach them. Practically every student goes from us today uninstructed and ignorant of exchange, currencies, commerce, and the part which gold and commodities must play in maintaining credit and world trade. Not only are we ignorant of these matters, but as a people we have become the victims of the grossest and most inexcusable exploitations. Practically everyone possessing any money at all in recent years has bought, often on what was apparently good advice, stocks and bonds to provide for his old age or his dependents, only to learn that those who advised him to buy were quite as ignorant of the value of the paper they were selling as he was himself. How the mighty have fallen! Great captains of industry are seeking release from their angry stockholders by death or exile, leaving in their wake the devastated hopes and destroyed ambitions of thousands upon thousands of persons.

To ignorance of government and of economics must be added ignorance of tariffs and international relationships. Do the American people know what tariffs really are, how they affect trade generally, and what the consequences of them are upon every phase of business in American life? Do they know how militant nationalism will affect the standards of living and the possibilities of international peace? The nations of the earth have built tariff walls around themselves that stand like jagged dragon's teeth, behind which the people are hiding. Thus they are creating new forms of selfishness and laying new bases for world wars. Should not the universities make it clear that the salvation of the nations of the earth lies more in their interdependence than in their independence? Must we wait to educate a generation of youth in these matters, or shall we undertake to reach the masses through extension services of the universities? That is something the state universities are peculiarly adapted to do.

State universities maintain that, in addition, they are faced with the obligation of promoting the economic rehabilitation of the areas in which they reside. Closely associated with business, industry, and agriculture, they are constantly engaged in replacing worn-out processes with new ones, so as to prevent the complete breakdown of agricultural, industrial, and economic life. We know that science destroys that which she produces by producing something better or something that can be produced more cheaply. We know that all around about us there are industries, forms of business, and agricultural pursuits passing out of existence because of new discoveries or new inventions. The pathway of the industrial life of America is strewn with the wrecks which science has made. If there were time I could point to a number of discoveries in the laboratories of scientific men of this country and abroad that will, in the next few years, mean that many forms of business and of agriculture will disappear. The time has arrived when the scientific men need to paint a new picture and to tell a new story. It is a picture or story of the future. It is a story which will substitute hope for despair, optimism for pessimism. It is a story of research programs which will aid in the economic rehabilitation of America.

It will not be sufficient to confine our efforts to research designed to help with the economic restoration of our country. There is great need for the study of a number of other important problems, such, for example, as taxes and taxation, investments, and the utilization of land, for millions of acres of land in many states are reverting to the states because of tax delinquencies, thus creating new public domains. And especially is there need for solving, if it is at all possible, the unemployment problem. All of which means that the university should be the one center to which the people of the state could and would look for unbiased, disinterested knowledge and consideration of public questions.

I saw the state universities of Australia performing this service. The most dramatic illustration was the balancing of the Australian budget. For twenty years Australia had been living on an unbalanced budget. She had been paying her interest by borrowing more money and by creating heavier debts from year to year. Then the crisis came. She could borrow no more money. She could not meet her interest obligations nor maintain her government. Thereupon the political leaders, not knowing where else to turn, did something unique in the annals of world politics and education. They sent for the professors of political economy in the various state universities.

These men, who already knew more about the economics of Australia than all the politicians combined, came with their charts, pooled their knowledge, prepared additional charts and maps, and then they in turn did something unique — they invited the premiers of the various states, including the premier of the dominion, to attend a short course and be instructed in the simplest lessons of economics. The bills that needed to be passed by the federal parliament and the various state parliaments were written by the professors and carried back by the premiers to their respective parliaments, which passed those bills without change in every instance except one. That was in New South Wales, where the premier changed the bill for political reasons, with the result that the budget of that state remained unbalanced until this premier was dispossessed of his office.

Perhaps it is too much to expect that America will place such reliance upon her universities, but signs are not wanting that many of the states are calling with increasing frequency upon their universities for assistance in the solution of their problems. The life, spirit, and work of the state universities are deeply affected and colored by these practical demands. This relationship, which inheres in the very purpose and nature of the state institutions, I would accentuate. If they are faithful to their purpose and to their constituencies, the state universities will be dynamic institutions to which society will look with increasing frequency and pride for advice and assistance in political and economic affairs, as well as in the consideration of things of a purely intellectual character.

All social engineering must rest eventually upon some education. It is infinitely better that social change should be guided by trained and informed intelligence than by untutored emotion or uninformed politics. And therein lies the challenge of the new day for the universities.

AN ADDRESS ON THE FIFTIETH ANNIVER-
SARY OF THE FOUNDING OF THE
UNIVERSITY OF NORTH DAKOTA

Grand Forks, North Dakota, February 22, 1933

O N THE earliest maps the territory of Dakota
was in that vast area known as the Great
American Desert. By 1832 George Catlin,
explorer, hunter, and artist, had spread the fame of the
regions later included in Dakota and made it known
even in Europe as an area of abundant sweet grass,
unlimited herds of buffalo, and fierce but handsome
Sioux Indians. By 1849 Dakota had been included
in the territories of five states, successively: Indiana,
Missouri, Michigan, Wisconsin, and Iowa. Then it
passed to Minnesota in 1851. After the treaty of Traverse des Sioux the legislature of Minnesota created a
colossal Dakota county, stretching from Lake Pepin
to Yankton or beyond. Its remnants still form a Minnesota county just south of the Minnesota River near
Minneapolis and St. Paul. It was said of this county
that the sheriff was free to chase a horse thief from
the Mississippi River to Fort Pierre. Inasmuch as un-

der the present division of states the sheriff would be operating in South Dakota, perhaps it is safe to mention this matter in Grand Forks.

I am bringing you no news when I say that Dakota Territory was split off from Minnesota when the state of Minnesota was organized in 1858, and that from then on until 1889, when the two Dakotas were admitted as states, the vast region originally comprised by the Dakota Territory was a single unit.

More than most people realize, Dakota has its place in the romantic pioneer history of the great West. Its great plains, its unbroken areas of fertile soil, its wild game, but even more especially its rivers, assured it of this fame. Historically the Red River of the North has been a connection with the great Scotch settlements that have developed into Winnipeg and the province of Manitoba. These waters flow into the historic Hudson Bay, a region that has remained romantic to the present day. Westward the Missouri has been from the first a legendary trail, stimulating to the imagination, and important as the route of Lewis and Clark, of fur traders, buffalo hunters, Indian fighters, and later of the cattleman, the sheepman, and the grain grower.

Much as we should like to recount the story of the heroic struggles of pioneer people who conquered this land with the implements of civilization, we must remember we are not assembled here today primarily to celebrate the founding of a state, but rather to celebrate the fiftieth anniversary of the University of North Dakota. It is difficult, indeed it is impossible, to dissociate the founding of the university from the character of the people who founded the state. Before the territory had reached the maturity of statehood, the plainsman and the plowman were thinking of the youth and were dreaming of the future. Already inspired by the American doctrine that education is essential to a free people and that a university is fundamental to the cultural and economic life of a commonwealth, their earliest acts were to establish a system of public education and a university. Today we are not concerned with their mistakes, for we know now that they weakened higher education by decentralizing and distributing its units too widely over the state. We are concerned with their achievements, one of the greatest of which, I venture, time will show to have been the founding of the university. This took place in 1883. The doors of the university were opened in 1884, well within the memory of living men. Its first faculty consisted of four instructors — a president who was professor of metaphysics, a vice president who was professor of natural sciences, an assistant professor of Greek and Latin, and a preceptress and instructor in English and mathematics. One cannot read this list of teachers without being impressed by the fact that the university was dedicated from the beginning to the improvement of the cultural life of the people. Seventy-nine students, all below the level of college grade, entered the institution the first year.

From these humble beginnings the university has grown, not without a struggle, to its present proportions. One can scarcely forego calling attention to the sacrifices that were made in early days to establish and to maintain the university and to wonder whether we are doing as well in these days.

The University of Minnesota has had many opportunities to learn of the quality of work of the University of North Dakota. Many of your young people come to the University of Minnesota, especially for graduate work. We know how well grounded they are in the subjects they study. On the other hand, not a few from Minnesota attend the University of North Dakota. We know how well this institution has fitted them for the practice of some profession and for citizenship. We have on our staff a number of your ablest graduates. And we, on the other hand, have contributed twelve members to the staff of the University of North Dakota.

Surely North Dakota should be a good state to live in, for we find that 110 graduates of our medical school, 85 graduates of our college of dentistry, and 135 graduates of our law school are practicing in the state of North Dakota. Your people should be healthy and should have a high sense of social justice. We have done what we could for the intellectual and moral improvement of the state. We wonder sometimes whether it is the education these leaders have received or the ozone you breathe that produces so many social and political experiments in North Dakota, the most recent of which is the suggestion that you secede from the Union. Much as we love you, I fear we shall not be able to join you in this undertaking!

Jesting aside, it must be clear that nothing but an imaginary line separates our states. We are the descendants of the same pioneer stock and are controlled by the same destiny. I feel quite at home in this university, for it expresses the same hopes and dreams that the university with which I am connected expresses.

I should not feel strange if I were speaking before any other state university group, for the conception of public education, including the state university, is deeply implanted in the political principles and philosophy of the American people. The pioneer founders of the American republic were of the opinion that popular government could not endure without popular education. George Washington emphasized this point in his farewell address; John Adams in 1785 declared that the whole people must take unto themselves the education of the whole people; Daniel

THE STATE UNIVERSITY

Webster in 1837 said, "Let no man have the excuse of poverty for not educating his offspring"; Thomas Jefferson established a university "in which all the branches of science [i. e., knowledge] deemed useful in this day shall be taught in their highest degree." The conviction that there could exist no political equality without equality of opportunity guided the thought and directed the action of the early political leaders. But these statements remained as mere expressions of sentiment until, at a later date, there was added to them another: "Every career should be open to talent."

With the plea for wider opportunities based upon differences in talent came the movement to establish state universities. These institutions did not come into existence without effort, nor were they without critics. But Jonathan Turner, Abraham Lincoln, Stephen A. Douglas, and other distinguished public leaders gave strength to the cause by passing the Morrill Act, giving the land grant colleges and universities the most magnificent endowment ever granted by one law by any political body. The critics who opposed the establishment of the universities offered arguments some of which seem strangely familiar in these times. They said, "The state is not competent to control the subject of education." They spoke derisively of the institutions as "splendid nightmares," or "utopian schools," "admirably calculated to ease the state of a few millions, and establish a state farm where some salaried and skillful professors, twirling ebony canes and shaded by silk umbrellas, might teach some would-be farmer (all but the labor) how to farm scientifically."

But this cynicism did not prevail. The schools were established, and with magnanimous purposes. Professor Bernbaum of the University of Illinois, referring to these purposes, says, "The new type of university had in view nothing less than ultimately making *every* human occupation a learned one, in the sense of basing it upon knowledge and intelligence, and of opening to *every* man and woman the opportunity of bettering his condition of life."

It would not be without profit, if we had the time, for us to speculate upon a social order in which every human occupation is based upon knowledge and intelligence, and where every man and woman looks upon education as a means of bettering his life. But such a speculation would take us too far afield from the considerations to which we should give our attention at the present time. That no state university has fully achieved these high purposes we may safely admit; that they represent hopes to which every university may aspire within the limits of its support we may likewise agree. We know all too well that human history is filled with the stories of institutions that were founded upon sound principles, yet have sunk into insignificance or ruin because their supporters disregarded their ideals or fell into ways of living that slowly but surely undermined their purposes. It requires high courage — the courage of which pioneers are possessed — to upbuild and to preserve the integrity of the institutions of democracy. Courage of this high type is particularly needed for the universities if they are to survive and to serve the children of the men who sacrificed so much to found them.

Never were universities in greater need of moral support than now. In the effort to extricate ourselves from our present economic distress there is grave danger that we shall destroy the sources of our hope and the springs of our recovery. We have not learned in America to respect the scholar and to use his knowledge in disposing of our problems. When we are in trouble we appeal to politics rather than to intelligence. And politics continues to play fast and loose with human misery, regardless, it seems, at times, of public interest and of human welfare.

I do not need to remind you that the present depression is the worst we have ever experienced. It is more severe; it is more universal; and it affects the agrarian population of the world more desperately than any we have ever known. The average citizen in his desire for relief has reached that state of mind where he is looking for fellowship in suffering. I heard a story recently of a group who were talking about the depression. They talked on and on, each one becoming more and more vehement in his castigations of everyone who had anything, until they reached the point of wishing that nobody had anything. One member of the party, thinking that the conversation was being carried too far and desiring to change its drift, turned to a boyhood friend of his whom he had not seen in years but who still lived in the home town, and asked, without regard to the subject they were discussing, "Charley, how is the old church back home these days?" But Charley was not able to free himself from the spell of the talk; leaning forward, with face drawn and body tense, he said, "It's in a terrible fix, a terrible fix, but the Congregational church is worse, thank God." So long as we rejoice in the suffering and privation of others we shall never recover from our present distress.

Most people do not realize that America is making a great decision. It is a decision as to what her future course shall be. If she continues to follow the course that she has been following since 1929, it will mean greater national isolation, a lower standard of living, and peasant workers and peasant farmers. Surely none of us looks forward with equanimity to that situation. Most of the things we have done to date have furnished us with temporary relief and have buoyed us up for a time, but they have not solved our problems. The decision we are making is whether we shall continue to do things that reduce us to lower and lower standards of living, destroy the birthright of our children, and blast our hopes and ambitions generally. I sometimes wonder how long the youth of our country will support us — to the point, do you think, where the historian of the future will speak of them as "the lost generation"?

Why do we resort to these expedients? Partly because of our political leadership, partly because we do not know what to do, and partly because we are unwilling to accept the leadership of our scholars. In days of prosperity we refuse to accept the leadership of our scholars because they are not prosperous; in times of depression we refuse to follow them because they are public servants. We do know that life has become complex and its problems difficult and even subtle. That we do not know what to do with many of these problems we readily admit. Even the terms associated with many of them often carry no clear meaning to us. Do we know, for example, what the gold standard really is and what part it plays in determining international credit? Do we understand how the fluctuations in foreign exchange affect trade? Are we familiar with the effect of trade quotas upon American trade? Are we clear about the influence of intergovernmental debts upon world recovery? One group advocates the inflation of currency or credit, another the deflation of currency or credit; one proposes a limitation of agricultural production under governmental control; another the fixing of prices on agricultural products; and so on throughout a long list of suggested panaceas. The truth is we are still listening to the Pollyanna stories of the uninformed. And yet we are in the midst of war far more devastating than the World War of a few years ago. The instruments of that war were guns and gas and battleships; the instruments of the present war are tariffs, fluctuating world currencies, trade quotas, foreign debts. We knew what to do when we used guns and gas and battleships; we knew how to reach the enemy and to rout him from his place of concealment. We do not know how to use the instruments of this new war; we do not even know where the enemy is. We are learning too slowly and at an enormously heavy cost.

America is a proud country. Her spirit was rather admirably described the other day by the head of one of our great financial corporations, who said that the thing for America to do is to smash the economic gates of other nations. We are in great danger of learning too late that this cannot be done. We do not belong to the League of Nations, we have not joined the World Court, we send our protests to Japan, we rear high economic boundaries, we suggest to the rest of the world that it buy our goods, desiring at the same time to avoid buying its goods so far as possible. Yes, America stands alone. There is no place in the world where she is more highly thought of than she is at home.

The distress in which we find ourselves cannot be attributed to the universities of America nor of the world. John Maynard Keynes, the great English economist, wrote a book about ten years ago in which he foretold what was ahead. The business and political leaders scorned his advice. Now he has written another, the theme of which might be said to be "I told you so." Again, a thousand American university scholars in the field of economics urged the president of the United States not to sign the tariff bill. But the business and political leaders urged him to sign it, and he did. And the press of the country scourged the professors for venturing to have any opinion on the subject. Time and again since then, little groups of scholars have ventured feebly to express their views on some public matter only to be promptly chastised and put in their place.

No, the universities of America never taught national isolation, they taught international cooperation; they never taught the breakdown of foreign trade, they taught the necessity of building it up; they never taught war, they taught disarmament and peace; they never taught the things that will impoverish, rather they taught the things that will enrich a people. We are where we are largely because we have disregarded what we have been taught and because we persistently refuse to avail ourselves of much of the knowledge at hand that might help in the present emergency. If the knowledge needed to dispose of the grave problems now awaiting solution is not available, then clearly we should concentrate the energies of governmental and educational agencies upon the study of those problems, for solutions should be based upon facts rather than opinions.

But we in the Northwest do not need to wait upon the nation before we begin the consideration of some measures that will assist materially with our recovery. This much seems perfectly clear: either the farmers must produce less, or new markets must be found, or new uses must be created for what they produce. With the first two of these alternatives we shall not concern ourselves further today, but the last, that of finding new uses for what we can produce, is not only a matter of supreme concern but something to which universities can and should be expected to devote a large share of their effort. History shows that science has destroyed many phases of agriculture in the last seventy years by its discoveries. History also shows that science has found many new uses for agricultural products during this same period.

In this connection we are reminded that Minnesota and the Dakotas are parts of the same economic area. They are served by the same railroads, interested in the same agricultural and financial problems, and populated by the same kinds of people, and they are making common cause in the building of this region.

An example of these common interests may be found in the instance of the extensive North Dakota lignite deposits. Your division of mines here at Grand Forks has done some important research in the utilization of these deposits. Scientists at the University of Minnesota are interested in them also. They see, as one possibility, the use of pulverized lignite as a basis for an iron industry in Minnesota, employing cheap fuel and low-grade iron ore from the Mesabi Range. Recently, also, a group of scientists at Minnesota has become interested in the possibility of obtaining cheap and abundant fertilizer for the agriculture of this Northwest region from North Dakota lignite, from Montana phosphates, and from Minnesota peat. The need for fertilizer to rehabilitate the soil is well known. Unless the soil is rehabilitated, its productivity will soon amount to almost nothing in great sections of this area. The day is fast approaching, if indeed it has not already arrived, when we cannot save the railroads nor ourselves with doles from the Reconstruction Finance Corporation.

But it may be asked, Why should we try to increase the fertility of the soil when more goods are being produced than can be sold? For example, there are some sixty million bushels of low-grade grain in the elevators of this region now that we are unable to dispose of. The point is that we must find new uses and new values for this grain. Hitherto it has been used chiefly as food for human beings and animals. Now it must be used for something else or it will constitute a constant glut on the market. Our scientists say that if they are given reasonable support these uses can be *found*. There are many chemicals in these grains; these elements can be separated and commercial uses can be *found* for them. All this we know to be practicable provided we do not lose our scientists and provided we support them. They maintain, and not without good reason, that they can show how new uses can be found for at least twice as much as we are now producing. This will call for better soil, more fertilizer, a more extensive use of lignite and phosphates. This means more work, less unemployment; more wealth; less poverty.

This is only one of a dozen illustrations that can be given showing how important economic results are dependent upon science and how intimately these results are related to prosperity in this region. Americans have never been willing to "gamble," so to speak, on science as a basis for commercial prosperity. It is true that we have spent — that is, private business has spent — large sums; but democracy as such, i. e., the federal and state governments, has not spent much. Germany spent five million dollars on researches on dyestuff. She put all her government and university laboratories to work on the problem with the result that she soon had a monopoly of the world trade in that field. This is what America needs to do; that is what each of the states needs to do. One road to recovery can be opened by the test tubes and microscopes of the scientists.

The time has arrived when we should turn our thoughts to the future and forget the past. Much of what we once had is lost; it is gone forever. We can rehabilitate ourselves only by doing something different. If we think of the past we despair; if we think of the future we take on new hope. We should substitute the doctrine of regeneration for the calamity talk of disintegration. There are things to be done that will lead us out of the morass in which we find ourselves. The universities have a part, indeed a conspicuous part, to play in the new drama that lies ahead. They can do their part only as they are respected and encouraged in their work.

A wise democracy will not wait; it will plan for a new day, and its plans will be radiant with optimism. If we take a new grip on ourselves and maintain that a new day has just begun, it will, I dare say, soon begin. Let us be more like youth, that takes its counsel of hope. It refuses to throw aside the freedom of a new world for the servitude of the old.

The editor of the *Atlantic Monthly* says, "To the historian ours will seem the record of a vacillating and inharmonious people. We have watched England fight against her poverty as a century ago she fought the Peninsular War, with unremitting courage. We have watched France win the battle of the franc as she won the battle of the Marne. For good or evil, we have watched the integration of Italy and of Russia, fashioning worlds out of new elements. But where is the stamp of the American character in the times we live in?"

We insist that America possesses great qualities necessary to the salvation of democracy. We think the greatest of these lies in the pioneer spirit that built America. We sing the praises of those who dared to go into an unknown country, there to establish homes and to build a civilization for themselves. We thrill with the stories of pioneers who went with gun and knapsack, only to be followed later by itinerant minister and teacher and settler, into new lands in search of new treasures. Those days are gone. The frontiers we face today lie in the intricacies of our complex social organism. They open the way for new adventures and new hopes. To conquer these frontiers of our day the instruments of science must be used. Those who use them will be honored in their day and by their descendants even more than those who first broke the sod of new territory are honored now. In that vast territory which now seems to us so blank, the greater universities and colleges will gradually enlarge their influence and spread the patterns of a rich national culture and a prosperous economic order.

What better time, what more propitious time can there be than the fiftieth anniversary of this university for the people of the state to review the purposes for which it was established, for the people of the state to reincarnate in the university itself the pioneering spirit which looks ahead to achievements not yet performed, to deeds not yet done, to victories not yet won!

CONFLICTING GOVERNMENTAL
PHILOSOPHIES

An address delivered before the Department of Super-
intendence, National Education Association,
Minneapolis, February 27, 1933

E VEN in times of peace there is a conflict between the dominant world philosophies, and in times of war or of distress and unrest the conflict assumes proportions of great interest and significance.

We are accustomed to think of the instruments of war as ships and gas and guns. These are the instruments that nations usually use in their efforts at conquest. We all know of the terrible loss of human life, the bankrupt treasuries, subjugated governments, broken homes, and untold suffering that follow when these instruments of destruction are used.

But a war quite as devastating is sometimes carried on between nations with instruments far more subtle, yet quite as powerful and destructive in their influence. We are in the midst of such a war at the present time. It is an economic war, the instruments of which are tariffs, trade quotas and allotments, and deflated currencies. This type of war destroys the financial equilibrium and credit, which in turn results in the failure of banks, insurance companies, railroads and businesses of every kind. It unbalances public budgets, produces unemployment, impoverishes the people, and blasts the hopes and ambitions of everyone.

In our effort to banish these two kinds of war we seldom pause to consider that the controlling philosophies of the peoples of the earth are likewise contending for supremacy. Fascism, communism, militarism, democracy are something more than mere slogans. True, those who use the terms do not always know what they mean, yet they would lay down their lives to preserve their faith. When the world was small and communication was difficult, the political faiths and beliefs of distant nations received casual and belated attention in other countries; now we know of happenings in every part of the world a few hours after they occur. Our interest in the black shirts of Italy, the followers of the red flag of Russia, the Nazis of Germany, the armies of the militarist autocracy of Japan, has deepened. And when we observe that what they believe is affecting life and thought in other countries and in our own we begin to manifest still more concern in their beliefs.

The elements of conflict inhere in the divergent nature of the social theories upon which the political structure of the various nations is founded. Traditionally, racially, historically these theories flow out of different backgrounds and develop for different reasons. That should not blind us to the fact that the human mind is flexible enough to embrace any doctrine that promises better things.

With two of these world theories I have had intimate contact in the last four years — the communism of Russia and the militaristic monarchy of Japan. In 1928 I joined a group of educators to visit Russia. Some members of my board thought I should not go; a number of citizens were of the opinion that school teachers should not be allowed to visit a country that holds such extreme theories as Russia, and even the federal Department of Justice investigated the character and the views of the members of the party. When they found nothing especially incendiary about any member of the party we were allowed to leave the country, but with no visas to Russia and with no assurance that our government would protect us.

On the way over on the boat, one liquor-drinking judge from the vicinity of Chicago was especially loud in his condemnation of the party. He maintained that our primary purpose was to teach the Russian doctrine to the children of America. Neither he nor many others like him could understand, nor be made to understand, that our interest was the interest every American should have. Here was a people engaged in a new experiment in nation building — the most gigantic political experiment ever undertaken by any people, an experiment which in theory as well as in practice was opposed to practically everything we believe in and hold dear in America. Private property had been swept away, the church had been destroyed, the individuality of everyone was submerged in the common welfare of the state, the real control of the country was lodged in the hands of two million carefully and secretly selected persons who constitute the membership of the Communist party. It is difficult for us to conceive of a country in which no one owns anything, where farming is conducted on a majestic scale by the state, where the stores, the hotels, and the railroads — everything — are government owned and regulated; where capitalism has disappeared.

The Russians maintain that the capitalistic doctrine breeds selfishness, envy, hate, war — that it is, in fact, un-Christian — while the communistic doctrine, which means that there are no rich and that each does the thing he likes to do for the personal satisfaction he gets and the good he may do for others, is true Christianity. They point out that under the old order of capitalism and the church the Russian was kept in ignorance and comparative slavery, while now education is provided for him and his children, and, comparatively speaking, he has more liberty than he ever enjoyed.

For the old state church, which was rotten to the core, communism has been substituted. The old ikons of corrupt religious leaders have been taken down, and pictures, busts, and sayings of Lenin have been substituted. Everywhere Lenin is regarded as the great leader, the great emancipator, revered and worshiped by the people.

Wise in their day and, perhaps, foreshadowing what other nations must do, the political leaders of Russia are building future support by indoctrinating the youth with their theories. There are two million youths enrolled as Young Pioneers and two million more as Young Communists. One sees them everywhere with their caps, badges, and other insignia proudly displayed. Over the radio, by use of the movies, on the public platform, in the schools, these youths — all carefully selected — as well as the older generation, are taught to appreciate communism and to condemn capitalism. The imagination of the youth in particular has been captured by the trappings and symbolism of the cause they follow.

We in America have no real knowledge of what is going on in Russia; we do not understand this "new" philosophy, although it is really quite old; we speak depreciatingly, if not scornfully, of it. And yet it determines the way of life for one hundred and forty million souls, who are now trying to build a new utopia by political action, by industrialization, and by the processes of education. Nothing like it has ever been witnessed in all history. If the Russians succeed, what will it mean to the rest of the world? If they fail, what contribution will they have made to political and social thinking? These are questions to which we may well give an increasing amount of attention.

Russia is a land of strange contradictions. There the Orient and the Occident meet; there the meditation of the oriental is competing with the industrialism of western civilization; there you find decadent conservatism on the one hand and emergent liberalism on the other. Everywhere one meets with paradoxes. The schools, the press, and the public platform are all censored, and yet the people talk of the new freedom they possess. The chief controls of conduct are coercion, espionage, exile, and execution, and yet the people enjoy a pretended or an assumed voice in the affairs of the country. Stolid and ignorant, yet intelligent, the people are living under the spell of a new faith. Still, like dumb driven cattle, controlled through fear and spies and severe penalties, directed in all their activities, they somehow believe that they are right and all the rest of the world is wrong.

They are not satisfied to keep their theories to themselves. They tell the world what they believe in. They tell a new story and paint a new picture of the dreams of man. They find ready listeners in China and other parts of Asia, here and there throughout

Europe, and even in America. Wherever oppressed people exist, wherever men are suffering from blasted hopes and ruined ambitions, there the panaceas designed to produce a new social order take hold.

The grip that the Soviet doctrines have on the people of Russia was dramatically demonstrated last May Day, when a million persons marched before the dead leader Lenin as he lay exposed to public view in his tomb in the Red Square outside the Kremlin. The appeal these doctrines make is an appeal to an imponderable – a better life to be gained by discarding old institutions and by building new ones. The controls used by the governing classes are the controls of force rather than the controls of education and mutually sympathetic understanding. The life to be lived is a life dedicated to the common welfare rather than to the acquisition of property or social distinction or achievement.

A second of the great nationalistic philosophies to which I should like to turn our attention for a moment is that of Japan. A year ago I stood before the tomb of Meiji, the last of the great Shoguns, just as I had stood three years earlier before the tomb of Lenin. Meiji is to Japan what Lenin is to Russia and what Washington is to America – the great leader who stood for a new policy, designed to bring recognition and power and strength to his country. To his tomb come annually millions of pilgrims to worship. It was he who brought all the feudal lords of Japan under his dominion, created a new national ideal, and began to organize the Japanese empire.

We often think that Japan dates her rise to power from the time when Perry forced her to open her markets to the world. The real date goes back to the time when Meiji recognized the possibility of Japan's becoming one of the world powers and turned the face of his country from the East to the West. His emissaries visited every important country in the world. They brought back with them the things they could apply and make useful. Among other things they brought the military system Bismarck had devised, and imposed it without essential modification upon the Japanese people. There it exists almost without change to this day. It is not subject to legislative review but to the emperor only; it receives its appropriations directly from the emperor; and it rules Japan and determines Japanese policies with an iron hand.

The contrast between Japan and Russia is a contrast between efficiency and inefficiency, between cleanliness and uncleanliness, between a regard for traditions and a disregard for traditions. Both countries have programs; the Russian is clear and easily understood; the Japanese is hidden behind the inscrutable oriental countenance. One may judge what the Japanese plan is by the events of the last fifteen years. During this time Japan has been engaged in many campaigns, constantly acquiring new territory, and defying at the same time the League of Nations, the Pact of Paris, and the opinions of the nations of the earth generally. The Japanese program is, it seems clear, an imperialistic program involving the domination of the Orient.

Her military organization fears no country. It will, as national leaders told me, refuse to listen until all the nations of the earth speak in concert. The nations of the earth do not speak with one voice. Proud America speaks alone. She remains outside the League of Nations and the World Court. The diplomatic policies recently enunciated by America in respect to the Japanese at Shanghai and in Manchukuo have led many to believe that we are now trying to enforce upon the world the Monroe Doctrine, which we have hitherto applied only to the American continents. One cannot review these facts without being aware that the peace of the world is not yet secure. One experiences a certain feeling of futility when he makes this statement, for the whole world is still paying in distress and sorrow for the last war. And now we find it laying the bases for other world wars. What a heritage to leave to the next generation!

Russia seeks no new territory; she would like to destroy capitalism throughout the world. Japan seeks new territory; she hopes to preserve capitalism. Russia appeals to the emotionalized hopes of her people;

Japan to a sense of duty on the part of every citizen. In Russia everyone is supposed to work for the common good; in Japan the greatest honor a man can have is to die on the battlefield for his country.

In Japan, as in Russia, the press and public addresses are censored; academic freedom is not permitted to teachers; no one is allowed to speak disrespectfully or critically of the military organization; the instruments of control are force, imprisonment, and execution.

With Russia spreading her communistic theories and doctrines throughout the world by propaganda, emissaries, and agents, at a time when the whole economic structure of society is sadly shaken if not hanging in the balance, and with Japan, on the other hand, ignoring all the rest of the world as her armies pursue their way unchecked and unimpeded, every nation, and especially America, guided by a wholly different philosophy, should give constant and thoughtful study to these two theories of national life.

There is one other reason why we should give thoughtful consideration to these and the other national ideologies. Most of them, certainly fascism in Italy, Hitlerism in Germany, and sovietism in Russia, appeal to youth and undertake to dramatize its interests. They depend for their strength largely upon the enthusiasm of youth rather than upon the political significance of the movements themselves. Those behind the scenes, so to speak, may know what it is all about,

but the youth finds in these movements a moral exalta-
tion; their programs symbolize to him the rebirth or
reawakening of his nation. And it cannot be said that
the militarism of Japan is without its appeal to youth,
for it is closely and intimately related to the religion
of the country.

The zealous idealism of youth is a force always to
be reckoned with. Apparently the political leaders of
these countries realize that if you touch and mobilize
the moral enthusiasm of youth you have touched and
mobilized something of high potentiality. If you capture youth you capture the future. And these movements, in most instances, have swept into their organizations, like great consuming tides, the fresh and
sympathetic energies of millions of young men and
women.

Youth in most countries is resentful of the evasions
and dawdlings of its traditional political and economic
leaders. It is impatient with the old order of things.
Young people want something done about something.
They plead for action and social experiment. And
they are riding into power. Even in America the
younger electorate is dissatisfied with the formulae of
the old political parties. All that is lacking in America
for a new movement is a leadership that can, through
the very contagion of its personality and the character of its appeal, capture the imagination and awaken
the restless idealism of youth.

THE STATE UNIVERSITY

Every national philosophy is a way of life and of looking at life. In every instance the national ideal seeks to express and to perpetuate itself through education in some form. The kind of education that exists always reflects the national ideal or philosophy of the country. In Russia the schools are cooperative, party-controlled institutions; in Japan they are little autocracies; in America they are institutions in which individual effort and achievement are recognized and where individuals learn the lessons of social justice through participation. Democracy respects and exalts the individual; the other philosophies absorb him.

The chief means of control in a democracy, we have long believed, is some form of popular education rather than some form of coercion. We believe that the sovereignty of a free people resides in the exercise of a trained intelligence on the problems they have to face and solve.

America has maintained since early colonial days that there are just two guarantees of our civil liberty. One is the guarantee that all men shall have equal rights before the law, and the other is that they shall enjoy as nearly free and equal educational privileges as it is possible for society to provide. Our forefathers early discovered that an uneducated citizenry could not guarantee the dispensation of justice nor equal rights before the law. They turned to education to supply the corrective. They declared that the safety and perpetuity of a free government rests upon the level of trained intelligence among all the people. They saw that uneducated nations were nonprogressive nations, that ignorant people were superstitious and that they became the easy prey of the unscrupulous demagogue. So they established free schools to which the children of all people might go. This is America's contribution to civilization. Free education. becoming progressively more competent with the increase in the complexity of the social order, is America's contribution to the preservation of civil liberty. Equal rights before the law is an Anglo-Saxon guarantee, transplanted from European soil. Equal educational privilege is a guarantee indigenous to American soil. It seems clear that if we refuse to support either of these guarantees the other will fail.

We have prospered as no other nation in all history because, to some degree, we have kept faith with these ideals. Strange to say, we have kept the faith even in periods of our greatest depressions until this one. Now when we should be more vigilant than ever we propose to turn the clock back. During and immediately following each of the earlier depressions in America there was an educational reawakening which called for a revamping and a strengthening of the schools. Now under the stress of the breakdown of the financial structure of the world and under the pressure of many groups for tax reduction, legislative bodies, ignoring the democratic philosophy that has guided American life hitherto and disregarding the foundation guarantees of civil liberty, are striking more or less blindly at every tax-supported institution. Western civilization is hanging in the balance. She faces the past when she should be facing the future and moving forward to greater achievements. The truth of H. G. Wells's statement that civilization is a race between education and catastrophe has never been more obvious.

Of course there should be economy in the administration of all public institutions. And "economy," the word we hear so frequently these days, is nothing new in the schoolmaster's vocabulary. He has been practicing it for years, in fact, ever since he became a member of a self-denying profession. But very little of the waste and extravagance in public life can be laid upon the doorstep of the school teacher; certainly none of the graft.

If the political and economic leaders had followed the teachings of the schools, we should not be in our present difficulties. The schools never taught war, they taught peace; the schools never taught extravagance, they taught thrift; the schools never taught disregard for law, they taught respect for law; the schools never taught national isolation and selfishness, they taught international participation and cooperation. Now the people, as they strike out blindly to

248

save themselves from economic disaster, are about to wreck the schools, as if the wrecking of the schools would accomplish their end. We can find millions for highways, billions for public enterprises, hundreds of millions, if not billions, for a soldiers' bonus, but we must pare and scrimp on education. We are making helpless children and youth, in need of higher training for professional leadership, pay for our folly with shortened school years and inadequate equipment, under teachers whose salaries are being reduced to the point where continued professional growth will be impossible.

What is it that men want? They want the opportunity to labor, protection for themselves and their property, the right to educate their children, and all the comforts and conveniences society can possibly bring to them. For these things they are willing to struggle. Deprived of these things, sooner or later they will undertake to get them in new and strange ways.

When one contemplates these circumstances, he wonders what is ahead. He sees the foundations of democracy being undermined. He sees a clash of class interests in the offing, if indeed it has not already arrived. He sees the land, the mines, the railroads, the banks, and the public utilities all becoming government controlled if not government owned.

As he looks over the prairies of America, for example, he sees the farmers, once the capitalists of the country, now engaged in agrarian uprisings. He finds that the pioneer spirit flowing from ownership and freedom is still powerful among them. Now they fear losing their farms. Nor do they know why. They rebel and strike back, but not with the weapons that will save them.

As one looks ahead he observes that obedience to law has become a personal matter. He observes that we repeal laws today on the ground that we cannot enforce them, rather than on the ground that they represent an invasion of one's inherent liberties and constitutional rights.

I know I am out of tune with a great many when I mention these things. But I should like to be known in the years to come as one who tried to preserve rather than to destroy the traditions of America, as one who lifted his voice for a higher level of civilization for all classes rather than as one who supinely accepted the dictum that the days of opportunity have passed and the days of industrial slavery have arrived. I prefer to be known as one who tried, even though he failed, to strengthen the schools even in these days, for after all the only sure way the race has of making progress is through education.

Clearly the time has arrived when America needs to do some courageous thinking. She is making a choice, not by ballot but by the policies she is pursuing. She is choosing between recovery and stagnation;

between free classes exercising their independence and initiative, on the one hand, and peasantry on the other. Can it be that we think youth will willingly adopt a lower scale of living than their fathers have enjoyed? Do you see youth with affectionate resignation giving up the benefits and comforts of science, returning to the scythe on the farm, herbs in the practice of medicine, and the almanac for literature? Youth, we must remember, does not grow twice; even adults pass this way only once.

We think of Italy, of Russia, and even of Japan as engaged in social experiments. They have, each of them, a perfectly definite plan. America is experimenting, too, but without a plan. To say that America has done nothing or tried to do nothing to help herself in the present emergency would be a clear misstatement of fact. Most of the things she has done have been in the nature of expedients, designed to provide temporary relief but not to solve in any permanent way the problems we are facing. America is engaged in performing an economic miracle; she is trying to restore prosperity by reducing the purchasing power of everybody. We are doing our cutting first and our thinking afterwards.

That America will eventually recover we firmly believe. Her recovery may be the result of one hundred and twenty million people making ten million times ten million human adjustments, or it may be the result of social planning and of renewing the sources of strength and power. If it is to be by the latter method then there must be a renewal, a rebaptism of faith in the principles of our democratic philosophy. The instrument of democracy is the school. It is the great civic educator, superseding the autocrat, collectivism, and socialism, the army and the church. Its utility and necessity are now being subjected to new and more rigorous tests than it has ever experienced. At the very moment when we need to be strengthening it we find other world philosophies eating their way into the body politic and destroying the strength and stability of our own institutions.

If America is to grow in strength and influence it will be because she gives more, rather than less, attention to education; it will be because the gap between the scholar and the mass is bridged by a reorganized education; it will be because representative government represents thought, intelligence, and scholarship rather than the political ambitions of some officeholder; it will be because we build for the future; it will be because we adopt the gospel of hope rather than of despair.

To build a nation we should think of deeds not done, of achievements not yet won, of dreams not yet realized, of hopes not yet attained. Our struggle is still the struggle to attain liberty for a free people who shall be self-governing and self-directing. It is not the struggle to attain prestige for a nation by submerging the individual and controlling him through fear and coercion. "Lord God of Hosts, be with us yet, lest we forget" — forget that America can be made strong, her institutions virile, only as the youth of our day are fortified with knowledge and imbued with the necessity of preserving and upholding the guarantees of human liberty.

THE EFFICACY OF THE DEPRESSION IN PROMOTING SELF-EXAMINATION

An address delivered before the Institute for Administrative Officers of Higher Institutions, University of Chicago, July 12, 1933

T HERE is a common and rather widely accepted assumption that the depression has promoted self-examination among the colleges and universities of this country. This assumption arises out of the current opinion that society in general is experiencing a transformation of a fundamental and far-reaching character. Perhaps that is true, but the impact of deep-seated social changes upon social institutions is not always obvious, nor does it always express itself with equal effect upon all of them alike.

When one examines with care the reforms and the progressive advances being advocated in the field of higher education, he finds, for the most part, that their initiation antedated the beginning of the depression. The educational leaders of this country, long before the dark days of October, 1929, knew that their main problem was that of keeping their institutions abreast the needs of swiftly moving times. In this respect they enjoy unique distinction among the leaders of institutional life.

Some leaders cling with a tenacity born of tradition and conservatism to a social order whose decadency is obvious to everyone except themselves. There are others who hold with equal tenacity, and shall I say pertinacity, to the doctrine that the old order must be destroyed and a new one — one entirely new — must be created. The educator has held to neither of these views; he has seen society changing, its problems increasing in number and in difficulty; he has seen communities, states, and nations losing their isolation and becoming gradually more interdependent; he has believed that social change should not be left to drift but, on the contrary, should be the result of planning; now he beholds a new world — not clearly outlined, to be sure, but sufficiently clear for him to recognize that scholarship and science, both physical and social science, will play an increasingly conspicuous part in the preparation and administration of the plans of the new world order. It cannot be successfully maintained that the impress of these forces upon higher education is always clearly understood or recognized by the educator; sometimes he feels rather than discerns them, and in the feeling he experiences at times a sense of futility for fear that he should fail to make education serve the social needs that he sees passing in daily review before his eyes. The educator is not blind to these changes nor does he maintain that the schools are already doing all that can be reasonably expected of them. At no time has he lost sight of the fact that the schools, and especially the higher schools, are society's best instruments for advancing human welfare and that one test of their effectiveness is their sensitiveness to change.

One factor that has helped materially to bring about changes in the educational program is the enormous increase in registration in recent years. While it would not be without profit to inquire into the causes of this increase (for they lie, for the most part, outside the institutions themselves), we shall content ourselves with the thought that this influx of students, representing a wide range of mental ability and a still wider range of human ambition and interest, calls for adjustments in educational programs and for the introduction of new materials such as few contemplated a decade and a half ago.

These two sets of conditions, viz., a world of change and a new student body, when added to the tendency native to progressive educational leadership to look ahead, account for the fact that the schools were examining themselves before the depression put in its appearance. In fact, they were in greater ferment than they had ever previously known. They were testing and checking every aim, every process, and every result. They refused to worship at the shrine of tradition; they declined to accept any man's *ipse dixit* as to any educational theory. They were looking for facts that were true and for programs that would work. Many of their leaders were pragmatists of a high order. To these educators of pre-depression days the most important consideration about American education was that it must be constantly improving; it must not stay put – that would be a sign of weakness and of decay.

The depression merely accentuated this attitude; it did not create it. It is a fact that the urge forward is greatly stimulated in times of crisis; it is so now; we are in the midst of an educational renascence without knowing or being fully conscious of it. This renascence is not expressing itself in the same way everywhere, nor, indeed, is it manifesting itself everywhere.

To maintain that the depression has lifted all higher institutions of learning to a new level of exalted service would be far from the truth. Many of them have, in the face of declining incomes, watered down everything to the point of mere existence. What the ultimate effect of this will be, no one can tell. For some colleges and universities to retain their academic names at a time when they are but pale shadows of their former greatness, menaces to some degree the existence of all colleges and universities. For these institutions to claim that they are as good as they ever were will lead unthinking persons to believe that other more vigorous and more expensive institutions are in some manner deceiving the public.

The depression has wiped some institutions out of existence and it has sadly weakened others. So far as the state universities are concerned, it has had one other important effect. There has been a tendency, observed so far as I know for the first time, on the part of state legislatures to reduce the state university to the level of the most inadequately supported institutions of higher learning of the state. By this I do not mean to imply that the appropriation of the state university has been made the same as that of the most poorly supported institution, but that the same salaries are paid to all teachers in all state institutions alike. This has actually come to pass in a number of states. In North Dakota, for example, the salaries of all university teachers, of all normal school teachers, and of teachers in all other state-supported schools, have been fixed at $1,920 a year. The statement that a university teacher is no better than a teacher in any of the other schools was made in the legislature with telling effect. Nearly half a century of progressive and self-sacrificing endeavor on the part of pioneer educators to build a university of high rank is wiped out by a single act. The university is not destroyed, but it faces the danger of becoming ineffective. It will have difficulty — more difficulty than it has had in the past — in attracting and holding young men of talent. No amount of self-examination in which the faculty may engage can overcome the damage induced by the legislature.

North Dakota is not cited because she stands alone, but rather because the movement fully accomplished its purposes there. To a less extent exactly the same thing has happened in a number of other states. Many forces, of course, have contributed to this movement; the depression furnishes the most obvious explanation, but it does not fully explain what has taken place. In some of the very states where education was being curtailed beyond the point of healthy living, one often found the politicians creating political positions carrying salaries two and three times as large as the salaries paid professors. "Made work" of every kind under the guise of relief — sometimes there was genuine need for it, sometimes less need — was being created for every class except for the education of youth for leadership. Politicians appropriated millions to relieve the depression, new taxes were created, but not one cent more could be found to help aspiring youth fit itself for the consideration of the problems of its day.

In this connection I cannot forego saying that the depression has given the enemies of public education a more sympathetic audience than they have been accustomed to find. They have urged vigorously the restriction of registration to intellectually gifted students, assuming that educators are fully competent to pick such students at the beginning of their careers. The more extreme advocates of this doctrine go so far as to maintain that education above the graded schools should be paid for by those who are able to purchase it. In other words, they would deny the American doctrine that everyone should receive that type of education which is adapted to his capacities and needs. The outcome of this theory is easy to foresee; it means that the masses will be taught the rudiments of an education and that a small number of fairly bright people of wealth will receive the advantages of college training. Municipal and state universities will then disappear; a few higher institutions of a prestige character will survive and flourish. We should not pause to mention this matter here were it not for the fact that the desire to save funds — to solve the depression by reducing taxes, and especially the taxes hitherto made available for humanitarian and educational institutions — has made these critics vocal and respectable.

All universities and colleges have suffered more or less alike, the private institutions from a loss of income on investments and the state institutions from reduced appropriations. But it must be admitted, I think, that the state institutions have been more exposed to public criticism. They have been on the front line of attack. The people, in their frenzy to save themselves from complete economic disaster, struck out blindly, often without regard to the consequences of their acts

or the welfare of the institutions that had most to contribute to economic recovery and economic stability.
In some instances, to be sure, under the distress due to
bank failures, receiverships, and defaults, money to
support education, especially university education, on
a satisfactory basis simply was not available. Everywhere, however, there has been a noteworthy spirit
of cooperation among university people to assist in the
present emergency. Voluntary contributions by professors to help save the integrity of their respective
institutions have been common. This cooperation and
these contributions have been made generously and
willingly in the face of salary cuts in this country that
far exceed the cuts made in the salaries of university
teachers in many foreign countries and especially in
England.

The most obvious effect of the depression upon education has been the development of a concern about
the cost of education. Faculties have become budget-
wise. They have turned their attention for the time
being inward and have focused it upon expenditures.
Every item of expense is being subjected to the closest
scrutiny. Under the pressure of necessity faculties are
eliminating positions, alternating courses, consolidating departments, cutting down on equipment, enlarg-
ing classes, and discontinuing capital outlay. For the
most part these changes represent a struggle for sur-
vival. It would be unfair and unjust to claim that these

changes are activated by selfish motives; they are not. They represent an effort on the part of faculties to preserve as long as possible the inner essence of the institution.

In these attempts at curtailment the demand is not infrequently made that all nonessentials be eliminated. This is more easily said than done. The mere presence of so-called nonessentials is some evidence of their essential nature. If they are nonessential they should never have been established in the first place. Some of the types of activities listed as nonessential are the university press, the placement bureau, vocational and educational guidance bureaus, psychological testing, comprehensive examinations, and research bureaus. It will be observed that these are service functions of the university. To eliminate them means that universities must confine themselves chiefly to instruction.

Two groups of laymen recently called at my office to protest certain activities of the university. One group objected to the University Students Health Service and the other to the out-patient department of the dental and medical schools. Objection was made on the ground that these services produce an income. The position was stoutly maintained by the representatives of these groups that the university should engage in nothing that produces money. That, so they said, would mean that the university was competing with business or at any rate that it was securing revenue that should go to maintain doctors and others in the community. This was the first time I had ever been confronted with such a proposal. I asked them if they would have us abandon our dormitories and dining halls, for example. They said they would. I asked them if they would have us give up our control over the finances of the athletic department; they said they would. They were emphatic in their statement that our job is to teach, and that we should not maintain any agency that depends upon fees for support. Thereupon I asked them if we should not abandon all tuition fees of every kind, since Minnesota is in a sense in competition with the private colleges of the state. I called their attention to the fact that if we did that we should pass out of existence altogether. Then I discovered that they were alumni of the university and they did not wish to push the principle far beyond its effect upon them.

The impact of public opinion upon higher education has manifested itself in a number of other ways. As a matter of fact, it has affected higher education upon every level — national, state, and institutional. Some of the changes are merely sporadic; others may be fairly characterized as movements. An examination of these changes leaves one with the impression that higher education is undergoing changes of a sweeping and fundamental character. The future educational historian will look back upon this period as a time of transition in which education was revamped and reorganized to meet the needs of a new era.

There is a new deal in education as truly as there is in government. This new deal, as I have said, is revealing itself all along the line and on every level. We have recently witnessed a manifestation of it in the effort of the federal government to define more clearly its relation to education, including higher education.

It is well known that since 1862 the federal government has been assuming more and more responsibility for education on all levels. Its activities have been distributed through a wide array of departments, divisions, commissions, and boards. There has been no coordination of these administrative bodies. The sum they have expended amounts to tens of millions of dollars for higher education alone and to still vaster amounts when the lower schools are included. These various educational activities have been created by pressure groups. But there has never been a federal policy governing the educational program of the federal government. There has been no chart to guide it. Consequently its educational activities have continued to increase wherever pressure was greatest.

The need of a new appraisal and of outlining a fundamental policy for the guidance of the federal government in these matters was obvious. Everywhere there was confusion as to policy. New appropriations and projects were set up under special pressures to serve special needs. Overlappings of interest became more numerous, and the struggle for existence between groups became more intense. Federal control over state and local schools and over universities became more frequent. Fear was thus added to confusion. The result was that President Hoover appointed a committee, known as the National Advisory Committee on Education, to review these matters. In his annual message to Congress on December 3, 1929, the President said: "In view of the considerable difference of opinion as to policies which should be pursued by the federal government with respect to education, I have appointed a committee representative of the important educational associations and others to investigate and present recommendations." This committee consisted of fifty-two persons prominently engaged or interested in education. When the committee was organized by Secretary Ray Lyman Wilbur, he declared its purpose to be "to give us the proper chart by which to steer our educational course."

The report of this committee is one of the most important documents on education ever issued in America. It discusses for the first time in terms of fundamental principles the background against which public education should be evaluated. It presents a progressively expanding conception of public education in a democracy, shows how basic it is to the maintenance of liberty and to the exercise of sovereignty. It announces for the first time a series of principles that should serve as a guide for the federal government in future legislation relating to education.

The most fundamental of these principles as applied to higher institutions of learning is that the federal government should encourage but not control higher education in tax-supported institutions of America. There should be no regimentation of thought or of action. The enunciation of this principle, consonant with American philosophy since colonial times, was of vital importance; for the drift in the federal field in recent years had been in the direction of greater control. Through the appropriation of federal funds, control over education was being more or less subtly established. Research stations and types of education were gradually losing their adaptiveness; they became less sensitive to local and regional needs as they became more completely a part of a federal organization.

The necessity for a federal plan was accentuated by the depression. The government faced the necessity of reorganizing itself. It was seeking ways of balancing its budget; it was investigating all of its departments and activities. We may safely say that one of the most important results of the depression upon education has been the definition of a sound federal policy, which has now under President Roosevelt been adopted and put into action in certain respects.

Many of the states have found it necessary to do pretty much the same thing in outlining their relations to education. The survey movement, which dates back now approximately twenty-five years, was early made use of by a number of states to study the cost of higher education and the functional relations of the various institutions of higher learning. One state in particular, Montana, in 1913 went so far as to provide complete coordination of control. While various institutions still remained in existence, each maintaining its own autonomy under its own president and faculties, a chancellor in control of all the higher institutions of the state was appointed and a business officer in charge of the finances of the higher institutions of the state was provided. The arguments advanced in favor of this consolidation were that it would save money, reduce or avoid duplication of offerings, and that it would stimulate greater educational interest and achievement on the part of the institutions themselves.

This movement which resulted in the coordinated system in Montana provoked surveys in a number of other states. For example, Arizona, Texas, Kansas, Utah, Iowa, Missouri, Indiana, Wisconsin, North Dakota, and perhaps others had surveys made before the war.

THE STATE UNIVERSITY

I may be pardoned, I hope, for referring to the fact that I had the opportunity of participating in several of these. I was not always able to see at the time that they were bearing fruit. It seemed to me that there was a disposition on the part of both educators and laymen to lay them aside or to file them carefully away in the archives of the state capitol after the first wave of publicity had died down.

It is true, of course, that as one looks back now over long stretches of time, one is able to point to the introduction of certain policies that these surveys made possible. It is a mistake for one to expect democracy to become intelligent quickly and to act promptly upon the recommendations of experts. Sometimes results are slow in coming. Democracy likes to deal with things nearest at hand. It finds it difficult to set up remote goals and to strive to attain them.

My experience with some of these surveys is illuminating. I should like to refer to two in particular. In 1916 I assisted with the survey of the higher institutions of North Dakota. A careful study of these institutions was made, a report was prepared and published by the United States Bureau of Education. So far as I was able to discover, it never accomplished anything. Very little attention was paid to it. But the 1933 legislature of North Dakota found it necessary to review its higher education program with some care. It discovered that when North Dakota was admitted as a state, every community in the state having a population of 200 persons or more had a state institution located in it. When the state ran out of penitentiaries and reform schools, it began to establish schools, so that all sorts were scattered all over the state. Now it is believed that North Dakota cannot maintain all these schools on a satisfactory basis. Members of the legislature in their efforts to study this problem found the survey report of 1916 and used its arguments in their addresses before the legislature. Strange to say, most of the arguments were about as fresh and patent as if they had been recently written. Opposition, however, developed in carrying out the provisions of the survey. The school people of the state who were critical of the survey report spoke respectfully of the other members of the commission as they are now all dead and maintained that my willingness to subscribe to the recommendations in the report was due to my youth. The point is that nearly twenty years after the report was made, calling for the reconsideration of higher education in that state, many of the arguments are still good and people are now giving consideration to them.

I had another experience soon after I came to Minnesota that shows how important a part these surveys may play in the determination of teacher training departments of a state. In 1920 I was asked to make a study of the teacher training departments of the state of Minnesota. This study was published by the Rockefeller Foundation. The report was widely distributed. The net result was that the next legislature of Minnesota, instead of abandoning the departments in the high schools as I had recommended, increased the number and their appropriations. But the 1933 legislature found it necessary to consider the cost of higher education. My report came to light. Once again my name was uttered with respect in legislative halls. I must confess that I got something of a thrill out of all this even though it was thirteen years late.

But since the war and during the depression this movement for the overhauling of higher education within the various states has taken on new life. In four states in particular — Oregon, North Carolina, Georgia, and California — commissions have recommended the elimination of some of the higher institutions of learning, the consolidation of others, the centralization of authority, and a general reorganization of the whole program of higher education.

Unified control of higher education now exists in Oregon, Iowa, Kansas, South Dakota, Florida, North Carolina, and Georgia; and unified control of all public education exists in Idaho, Montana, North Dakota, and New York. More than thirty states have coordinated the control of the training of teachers. In most of these the board having control is the state board of education.

EFFICACY OF THE DEPRESSION

In two states — Maine and Oklahoma — movements have been initiated to provide coordinated state systems of higher education including all institutions of higher learning, public and private. The arguments advanced in favor of such a scheme are that all these institutions are supported out of social income and render service to society. In both states the program calls for concentration, intensification, and development of existing facilities rather than diversification or expansion into new fields. In Oklahoma particularly, the governor of the state has advocated the placing of the physical property of state institutions under control of a board of trustees appointed by the governor, the physical property of private and denominational institutions to remain under their own control, the creation of a board of regents that shall have jurisdiction over the policies and standards of all institutions, the limiting of the smaller colleges to liberal arts work, the concentration of the technical and graduate work at the university and perhaps in one or two other places, and the granting of degrees only upon examination.

Within certain institutions there has been some tendency to effect a reorganization with a view to reducing the number of colleges or schools or administrative divisions. The most outstanding example of this perhaps is that of the University of Washington, which reduced the number of schools from thirteen to four, the four being arts and sciences, technology, law, and the graduate school. Those eliminated were music, home economics, fisheries, fine arts, forestry, journalism, library, nursing, business administration. Four of these, I believe, recently have been restored.

The George Washington University has introduced a plan of reorganization which provides for a junior college underlying the senior college and all professional schools. The senior college is to consist of four divisions of study: languages and literatures, mathematics and physical sciences, natural sciences, social sciences.

At Minnesota a General College has been founded for those students who find it difficult to do the work as it is now organized in the other colleges in the university, for students who do not care to carry full work, and for students who enter with advanced standing but do not fit into the regular programs of the university. The General College covers two years — freshman and sophomore. It grew out of the desire to experiment with the reorganization of materials of instruction. The tendency has been marked in higher educational circles in recent years to differentiate the materials of instruction to such a degree that it is practically impossible for a student to secure an overview of any field. What he gets is attenuated bits of knowledge taught by highly trained specialists. If any synthesis takes place it is more largely the result of accident than of intention. The establishment of the General College at Minnesota is a definite attempt to reorganize the materials of instruction with a view to providing that general liberal training which students need and desire, and to bring the students directly into contact with living problems. Thus far the General College must be regarded as an experiment, but the results seem to indicate that it may have a permanent place in the reorganized higher education program of the future.

The most noteworthy reorganization attempted by any university is that of the University of Chicago, the general aspects of which are familiar to this group. The plan calls for a concentration of the freshmen and sophomore years in what is known as the "college," recently expanded to include the two upper years of the high school. Progress through the college is made on the basis of examinations. Attendance at classes is not required. Recognition is given purely for achievement. In addition to the general work available for all students, there is some concentration for those who expect to go forward with their educational careers. When these students enter the university they follow the lines of concentrated effort.

One cannot pass by this list of plans calling for the reorganization of higher institutions without directing attention to the Experimental College of the University of Wisconsin. This was organized and operated

273

under the direction of Professor Meiklejohn. It was his belief that it is possible to take a limited number of students, give them the freedom which an ideal group of scholars desires, concentrate their reading and study upon some period of history, as, for example, the Grecian period, arrange for informal discussions and conferences, and by means of personal contacts and the general atmosphere of the group itself, stimulate intellectual effort and attainment of a high order. It was his thought that concentration on a given period would result in unity of purpose, of material, and of effort. This plan possessed certain inherent weaknesses. One was that it attempted to interest the students in a period that was about as remote from their actual experiences as possible; and another was the assumption that the youth of this age can be left entirely free. This seems not to have been borne out by the Wisconsin experiment. By these criticisms I do not mean to imply that no benefit resulted from the experiment. Professor Meiklejohn's book describing the experiment is one of the most stimulating and constructive discussions of education ever written in English.

Nor can one pass by this list of projects without calling attention to the Institute of Human Relations which has been established at Yale. This again is an attempt on the part of college authorities to bring to bear upon current living problems all of the knowledge and interest of a higher institution. The study of unemployment in a given area in Connecticut, for example, calls for an analysis of the social background of the unemployed by the department of sociology, of the economic situation by the members of the department of economics, of the psychological attitudes, handicaps, and possibilities of the unemployed by the department of psychology, and of the vocational possibilities by some other department. In other words, sociology, economics, psychology, education, dietetics, medicine, psychiatry — these and related departments pool their knowledge, agree upon the techniques that should be used in the study of the unemployment problem in the Connecticut area, mass their effort, and undertake to reach conclusions as a result of their combined study. What they would do for a community corresponds to what a medical clinic would do for the individual. After the individual is thoroughly examined, the reports of the various departmental specialists are sent to a common center; there an analysis is made of them, the physical defects with which the patient is suffering are revealed, and remedies are suggested.

In the last three years nearly forty reorganizations of various kinds and degrees have occurred among American colleges and universities. These readjustments have been made in an effort to meet higher standards of organization and efficiency, to secure concentration of resources and more adequate support, to eliminate competition, to achieve economy in administration, and to readapt the educational materials to correspond to the capacities of the students and to the social needs of the times.

This paper would not be complete if I failed to call attention to two other movements that have received new impetus from the depression. I refer to the junior college and the adult education movements. I can make clear what I have in mind by referring briefly to Minnesota. We have 225,000 youth in Minnesota between seventeen and twenty-four years of age, about 82,000 of whom have graduated from high school since 1929. Of these not more than 25,000 or 30,000 are in college. Nearly 49 per cent of all those applying for jobs are between eighteen and twenty-four years of age. Although the high school registration is increasing and public school authorities are doing what they can to provide post-high school work, there are probably 180,000 unemployed youth in our state. Here is a great area of humanity from which the leadership of tomorrow is to come that is being left largely unprovided for by the various relief measures; but it is not being left untouched by the depression.

Two things are happening: communities are urging the establishment of junior colleges to care for those qualified to attend college, and programs of adult education are being devised for all, but especially for the great body of these young people not equipped to go to college. We shall hear more of these movements. If we fail to consider them we shall pay heavily for our neglect in the future.

In the foregoing discussion, which I know full well is incomplete, I have undertaken to show that the depression has produced self-analysis in the following respects: (1) a consideration of costs and an evaluation of practices in terms of those costs; (2) a centralization of activities and functions in the interest of greater economy and efficiency; (3) the facing of educational institutions to the future with emphasis upon living needs rather than upon tradition; (4) the tendency as well as the necessity of higher education to spread so as to include the great masses of youth not now being reached.